INSIGHT

VALENCIA

C000052759

Discovery
CHANNEL

APA PUBLICATIONS L

Part of the Langenscheidt Publishing Group

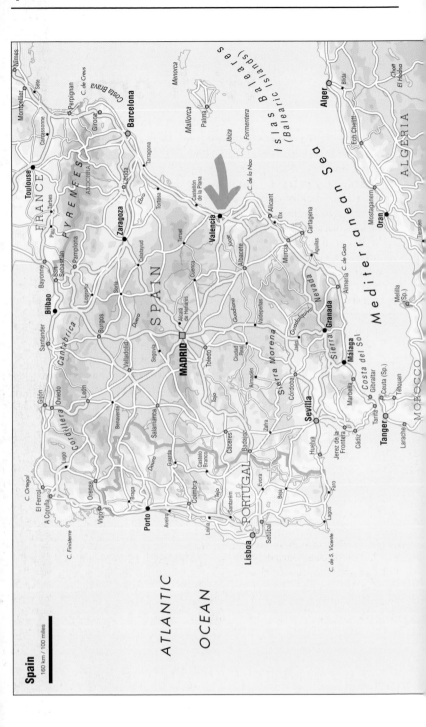

Welcome

his is one of 133 itinerary-based *Pocket Guides* produced by the editors of Insight Guides, whose books have set the standard for visual travel guides since 1970. With top-quality photography and authoritative recommendations, this guidebook is designed to help visitors get the most out of the city and its surroundings during a short stay. To this end, Vicky Hayward, Insight's writer on this area of Spain, has devised 14 easy-to-follow itineraries linking the essential sights and exploring some hidden gems.

The 10 city itineraries uncover the rich history that courses through Valencia, from its foundation over two thousand years ago to its contemporary status as Spain's third-largest city. These routes cover the old city, the new cultural sights, the docklands area and the beach. Four excursions to varied Mediterranean destinations within easy reach include the market gardens of the Huerta, L'Albufera freshwater lake, the ancient Roman town of Sagunt and the wine centre of Requena.

There are, in addition, sections on history and culture, eating out, shopping, and nightlife, plus a calendar of special events. A detailed practical information section towards the end of the guide covers transport, money matters, communications, etc, and includes reviews of hotels and accommodation possibilities in all price categories.

Vicky Hayward lives in Madrid, where she works as a features journalist, travel writer and book editor. She first visited Valencia as a child and has been returning to see friends there ever since. This guide shares the attractions that are, for her, key to the allure of this great Mediterranean city, from its historic and architectural wealth to its cultural riches, beaches, vibrant nightlife, enticing gastronomic scene and beautiful surrounding countryside. Vicky's special thanks go to Cristina Navarro and Antonio Ponce Lozano for inspiring her to write this guide.

HISTORY AND CULTURE

How Spain's third-largest city grew from a Roman retirement resort into a Muslim city-state, Balinsaya, surrounded by fertile market-gardens. Reconquered by the Christians, it was established as the capital of a kingdom within Spain. Thriving on its agriculture, craft industries and port, it has emerged today as a sparkling modern city by the sea......**11**

CITY ITINERARIES

contents 7

Preceding Pages: the view from Torres de Serrans; *fallera* costume
Following Pages: *las fallas de San José*

History & Culture

'This illustrious city…much larger than Barcelona, very well inhabited and settled, is found a little distance from the sea,' wrote German traveller Jerome Münzer in 1494. 'The Valencian people are very polite and affable…Merchants, artisans and clergy exceed two thousand.'

Münzer was writing at the height of the city's wealth and power, but his pen-sketch also gives a good glimpse of Valencia's character today. For it remains a vibrant city with a pleasure-loving Mediterranean spirit, a sharp-eyed flair for trade and a rich artistic legacy that never fails to impress.

When the city was founded more than two thousand years ago, however, the Romans had only modest plans for Valentia ('vigour'), a small farming colony, where war veterans could retire in a mild climate. But it flourished thanks to its natural advantages as both a safe port on a small island in a loop in the River Turia and as the crossroads where the main coastal high-way from Cádiz to Rome met the shortest route to central Iberia. By the 1st century AD Valentia's civic buildings were rivalling those of Saguntum, the other important Roman town on this central stretch of eastern Mediter-ranean coast. A temple to Diana stood on the site of today's cathedral, and next to that were the forum and thermal baths. Elsewhere were an aque-duct, a circus, taverns and villas.

As Roman Hispania's towns declined from the 3rd century, so Christian-ity grew to fill the vacuum. One of Valentia's church deacons, Vicente, was famously martyred on the wheel, making his home a pilgrimage shrine. During Toledo's Visigothic monarchy, Catholicism finally became the autho-rised religion, and a bishopric was set up. However, early in the 8th cen-tury the established order was overturned again. Arab and Berber forces swept into southern and central Iberia, and Valen-tia became a Muslim city, Balinsaya, for the next 500 years.

The Muslim City

Today, there is little to see of Muslim Balinsaya, since its great monuments – the riverside palace, the Albufat tower and its main city gate – were all pulled down in the 19th century. Nonetheless, its geography underlies today's city. As the city grew to fill the entire river island, different quar-ters developed. The main mosque stood where the church of Santos Joanes was later built and the market quarter spilled around the Plaça Redonda; north of that, a labyrinth of narrow alleys lined with houses and workshops ran to the riverbank, where the Barri del Carme stands today.

Left: 18th-century tiled frieze, Museu Nacional de Ceràmica
Right: Roman theatre at Sagunt

Muslim farmers developed the city's famland too, draining marshland close to the lagoon that they called the Albufera – the Little Sea. There, they planted rice, then a new crop to Spain and still today a star ingredient in Valencian cuisine. Over the centuries that followed, a vast network of irrigation channels was constructed. Fed by eight 'mother' canals, or *acequias*, it channelled water off the River Turia and around the plain's fertile farmland via thousands of brick watercourses. Lemon, orange and mulberry trees – the last for feeding silk worms – sugar cane, cotton, saffron, spinach, aubergines and watermelons, all newly introduced from the east, were planted

in a spreading green sea of orchards and market gardens.

In the 11th century, after the Cordoban caliphate collapsed, Balinsaya grew into an independent city-state *(taifa)*. This was a time of economic and cultural renaissance. Leather, paper and ceramic workshops flourished. Ceramics, which came in many styles and in forms ranging from water-bottles to tiles, called *azulejos*, have formed part of the city's decorative style ever since. Poetry flowered, too, establishing another tradition that is still alive today.

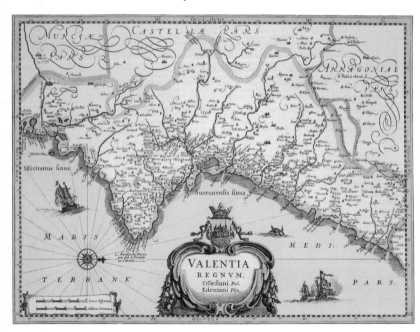

Top: El Cid takes Valencia from the Muslims
Above: a map of the Kingdom of Valencia, 1640

A stout wall was built to protect Balinsaya, but the city-state's wealth drew the eye of El Cid, the legendary Castilian mercenary warrior, who conquered it in 1094, becoming Duke of Valencia. After his death in 1099 his widow, Jimena, held the city for six years before it fell to Muslim troops from the North African Almoravid dynasty.

The Kingdom of Valencia

When Balinsaya fell to the Christians for the last time in 1238, it was to Jaime (James) I of Aragón. He allowed 50,000 of the city's Muslim residents to leave with their possessions within 20 days and to settle south of the nearby River Xúcar. The Muslims who remained, mainly craftsmen, moved to a separate walled area of town, known as the *morería*, close to the river. Jaime allowed the city to keep its independence, making it capital of the Kingdom of Valencia, which was part of the expanding Aragonese empire. For 450 years the kingdom was to have its own laws, its own currency, its own language and, later, its own tax-collecting service, the *Generalitat*, from which today's regional government takes its name.

The Reconquest changed the face of the city. Jaime turned the Arab summer palace into a royal residence, reserved the Albufera lake as a royal hunting ground and built a portable wooden wharf where today's docks stand. Each of the new Christian settlers – Aragonese knights, priests, monks, nuns and Catalan tradesmen and craftsmen – was given at least two small Muslim houses or land on which to build. Ten mosques were converted into churches, and an elected municipal council met in the Palau de la Generalitat.

But there were many continuities with the past. Muslims made up the majority of the region's population for another hundred years – and they stayed on here till the 17th century. The city also kept Balinsaya's water court for settling irrigation disputes, its bathhouses and its *mustaçaf*, a city official who ran the markets, highways, building and manufacturing standards. Paper- and silk-making continued to flourish and so did trade with North Africa. Muslim artisans working for Christians, known as *mudéjars*, included skilled craftsmen who created carved wooden ceilings, brick vaulting and geometric decoration in churches and palaces. Most important of all, the city's market gardens and rice paddies were still tended by skilled Muslim farmers who built them. Known as '*la regalada*', or the pleasant land, the countryside was renowned for its wealth, then, as now, showcased in the city's central market. 'What an aroma of fruits! What great variety, cleanliness and beauty!' wrote Valencian humanist Lluís Vives in his famous *Dialogos* (1492).

Vives' description captures the exuberance of Valencia's 'golden century', when it grew into Spain's largest, wealthiest and most cultured city. An

Above: Jaime I of Aragón (1213–76), founder of the Kingdom of Valencia

important financial centre and port, it had close trading links with Italy, France and Flanders and was home to a cosmopolitan merchant community trading fruit, vegetables, cloth, leather, ceramics, gold and spices. The greatest monument of the age was the cathedral-like Llotja, or trade exchange, which housed the municipal bank, called the Taula de Canvis i Depósits, a trade court and a debtors' prison.

The city's artistic flowering reflected its trading contacts and the patronage of the Borgia popes, descendants of the Borjas, who came from Xátiva, just south of Valencia. Italian artists who came to work here influenced local painters such as Joan de Joanes and Jacomart, and stonemasons such as Pere Compte, who designed the Llotja. Others, notably Luis Dalmau, evolved an Hispano-Flemish style. Their magnificent work filled churches, convents and monasteries. Literature flourished, too. Spain's first printing press was set up here in 1474 and others mushroomed after the university was established in 1502, helping to popularise Ausias March's poetry and Joanot Martorell's novels, both written in Valencian.

The thriving port helped turn Valencia into the affable open city discovered by Münzer. Its brothel quarter, or *partit*, close to El Carme convent, was 'a large and celebrated place full of girls dedicated to public pleasure', according to French priest Barthelemé Joly. Official fiestas included Corpus Christi's extravagantly costumed processions and masquerades; other fiestas ranged from mystery plays with choirboys dressed as angels, to Carnival revels with oranges thrown around the streets, to 'Moors and Christians' street battles and, on St Joseph's Day, the carpenters' spring bonfires.

On the Sidelines

It was the waning of religious tolerance that signalled the beginning of the city's long, slow decline. A Castilian army pogrom against the Jews in 1391 and a local attack on the *morería* in 1455 were warnings of greater trouble to come. The Inquisition's arrival in 1482, the expulsion of Jews a decade later and the Catholic church's campaign against Protestantism ushered in a new religious intolerance. The Muslims, few of whom converted, were increasingly blamed for problems ranging from plague to piracy. Finally, in 1609, the order was given for their expulsion. A quarter of the kingdom's population left in two years, and, in 1613, the city's bank, the Taula de Canvís, went bankrupt.

Natural disasters and governmental errors deepened the decline. One-fifth of the city's population died of plague between 1647 and 1652. Land was left untended, rents and taxes remained unpaid, and the craft industries slumped. Sixty years later, the Habsburg dynasty's failure to produce an heir led to the War of Spanish Succession, in which Valencia backed the wrong party. Felipe V, the victorious incoming Bourbon king, ended independence, making Valencia subject to Castilian laws, taxes and government. Troops were garrisoned in the city and crown appointees replaced the elected council.

But prosperity returned once Valencia's population began to grow again in the mid 18th-century. The silk industry brought wealth and lavish baroque architecture to both town and country. Silk worms were cultivated in farmsteads, and the raw silk was dyed and finished in Valencia and nearby towns such as Requena. At the same time Carlos III's reforms boosted trade and agriculture. Permanent docks were built in the port, the Albufera became farmland, and fishing families filled in the marshes. Urban reforms came, too. One law prohibited St Joseph's Day bonfires in narrow streets, so transforming them into larger spectacles in the city's plazas. These *fallas*, or bonfire sculptures, have given their name to the city's most important fiestas.

Industrial Boom Time

In the 19th century, Valencia, like other Spanish cities, was dogged by the long-running struggle between monarchists and liberals who favoured a constitution. In 1808, a popular uprising during Napoleon's occupation forced state officials to declare war on the French. Briefly but gloriously independent once again, the city's government survived till 1812. Ironically, it was also in Valencia that Fernando VII, returned from enforced exile, announced a return to authoritarian monarchy in 1814.

But politics were to have less impact on everyday life than the arrival of steam power and a new agricultural boom. The silk industry declined, but furniture-making, metallurgy and ceramics flourished, and oranges became Spain's biggest agricultural export. By 1900 factories were replacing workshops, the population had quadrupled to reach 215,000, and the first workers' unions were born. A wave of rebuilding followed the 1837 dissolution of the monasteries, which had occupied a sixth of the city's land. Another wave came

Left: El Carme's Renaissance cloister
Above: the 18th-century Palau de Dos Aigües. **Right:** a travel poster from 1930

after the medieval walls were pulled down in 1865. Travellers were shocked. The English writer Augustus Hare, who came here in 1872, wrote of the 'warfare against antiquities'.

Luckily, the late 19th-century building boom coincided with the flowering of the art nouveau movement – or *modernisme*, as it is known in Spain. Colourful ceramic friezes, fruit and fauna motifs and, later, classical statues and medieval turrets lent an air of fantasy to civic buildings. Home-grown *modernisme* also left a colourful mark on the modest seaside quarters behind the flourishing port. Alongside this grew the Renaixença, a movement fostering Valencian identity through literature, art and language. Its greatest figure, the novelist Vicente Blasco Ibáñez, spearheaded a reformist Republican revival, called *blasquismo*, which held sway in the early decades of the 20th century.

When Franco's Nationalist uprising triggered the Civil War, Valencia declared for the Republic and became its capital from 1936–37. By the time the city surrendered the day before the war ended in 1939, bombing had left extensive damage, especially in the port. Reconstruction took more than two decades, and work was set back when the river broke its banks in 1957, flooding three-quarters of the city and leaving thousands homeless.

A Reborn Region

When prosperity returned, it came quickly. After crowds of European sunseekers came to the region's beaches in the early 1960s tourist revenues fuelled industrial growth, property speculation and liberal ideas, which helped to make Valencia one of Spain's liveliest (and noisiest) regional capitals. Since the return of democracy, the regional parliament has guided the city's debates, remaining united on seeking greater decision-making power and supporting the comeback of the Valencian language. As Spain's third city continues to grow, a series of grandiose new urban projects, such as the City of Arts and Sciences, a 'macroport' and a revamped waterfront, plus the hosting of the America's Cup in 2007 and 2009 and Formula 1's European Grand Prix in 2008, have all helped to catapult it back to centre-stage. And as this regeneration takes place, the Valencians themselves revel, night and day, in the older pleasures of a great Mediterranean city.

HISTORY HIGHLIGHTS

c. 35,000–8,000BC Levantine cave paintings at Stone Age settlement in El Parpalló, near Gandia.

c. 780BC Phoenician traders settle on the Mediterranean coast and build a port north of Valencia's site today.

219–18BC Saguntum, capital of Iberian Edetania, is destroyed by Hannibal. Rome invades Carthage's Iberian territories and retakes Sagunt in 212BC.

138BC Valentia founded by the Roman consul, Junius Brutus.

75BC Valentia destroyed during civil war and refounded as walled city.

AD304 Christian deacon, Vicente, martyred by the Romans in Valentia.

555 Byzantine troops conquer Roman Cartago, but by 624 lose control of all territories to the Visigothic kings.

711–18 Muslims invade and conquer Catholic Visigothic Spain.

1022–61 Valencia becomes a *taifa*, or independent state, Balinsiya. Its governor, Abd-al-Aziz, builds the second city wall.

1094 Valencia captured by El Cid.

1102 Muslim rule begins again.

1238 Valencia surrenders to Jaime I, King of Aragón, after five-month siege and on 9 October he declares Valencia city the capital of the kingdom.

1239 Jaime I establishes in Valencia an independent legal system, currency and parliament.

1244 Treaty of Almazira. Valencia is absorbed into the Kingdom of Aragón.

1413 Birth of Joan Martorell, author of *Tirant lo Blanc*, the first novel written in Valencian.

1474–79 Castile and Aragón are united in a federal monarchy following the marriage of Isabel of Castile to Fernando of Aragón.

1483–98 Building of La Llotja, the city's commercial exchange.

1492 Conquest of Muslim Granada.

1502 Valencia University founded.

1519–22 Valencian revolt against the Castilian nobility and persecution of Muslim converts *(moriscos)*.

1523 Birth of artist Joan de Joanes.

1609–11 Expulsion of *moriscos*. Valencia's population falls by a quarter.

1707 Valencia's independent laws are revoked after defeat by Felipe V at Almansa (War of Spanish Succession).

1768 Castilian (Spanish) becomes Valencia's official language.

1808 Valencia rises against Napoleon (War of Independence).

1812 Declaration of parliamentary monarchy in Cádiz.

1852 Railway line built between Valencia city and its port.

1863 Birth of Joaquín Sorolla, painter.

1865 Medieval walls are pulled down.

1867 Birth of Vicente Blasco Ibáñez.

1931 Alfonso XIII abdicates; Second Republic declared.

1936–39 Civil War. From 1936 to 1937 Valencia is the seat of the Republican government; in 1939 Valencia and Alicante fall to the Nationalists.

1957 River Turia breaks its banks and causes serious flooding.

1975 Franco dies. Prince Juan Carlos is crowned King of Spain.

1981 Abortive military coup. Tanks appear on Valencia's streets.

1982 The Generalitat (regional government) sets up parliament in Valencia.

1986 Spain joins the EU.

1988 Metro begins operating.

2004 City of Arts and Sciences opens.

2007 The 32nd America's Cup is held in Valencia.

2008 Valencia hosts Formula 1's European Grand Prix.

2009 Valencia hosts the 33rd America's Cup.

Left: the showcase City of Arts and Sciences

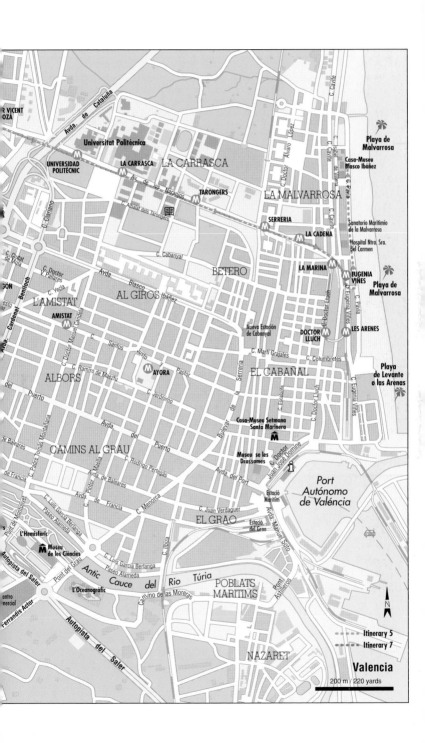

Valencia

200 m / 220 yards

Itinerary 5
Itinerary 7

Orientation

Even the shortest trip to Valencia will allow you to glimpse a city of many different faces. The Gothic quarter is the tightly packed nucleus of the old town that grew within its medieval walls until they were pulled down in 1865. To its north curves the dry bed of the River Turia and to the east, west and south spreads a spacious grid of 19th- and 20th-century tree-lined avenues and streets. The riverbed, edged by high-rise blocks on the modern north bank, is gradually being transformed into a green corridor of gardens linking the town centre to the futuristic City of Arts and Sciences. A tram ride east through the inner city's last surviving market gardens takes you to the port, the beaches and the old fishing quarter, which are now being extensively revamped.

Getting around between the different areas is easy thanks to fast, frequent and reliable bus, metro and tram services, as well as reasonably priced taxis. All the itineraries here combine public transport with easily walked routes. A car is not necessary and can even be a liability unless you want to explore the towns and countryside around Valencia. The majority of historic sites lie within the old town, where there is little public transport, and are within easy walking distance – the old town can be crossed in any direction in 25 minutes on foot. The street layout is confusing, so you will find that the pull-out map at the back of this guide is particularly useful. However, one of the great pleasures of Valencia is to wander and get lost in the old town's higgledy-piggledy streets.

Generally speaking, all the central areas are safe, but as in any city you should be careful in busy areas, such as the markets and the El Carme quarter, especially at night. During the sweltering high summer, it is more pleasant to do your exploring early or late in the day. The majority of cultural and historic sites are closed to the public on Monday, but the cathedral and churches remain open.

A Note on Language

The city's growing bilingualism means that its streets and roads, travel timetables, maps and sites are erratically signed in either Valencian, which is similar to Catalan, or in Spanish or, sometimes, in both languages. In this guidebook, all museums, sites, services and streets are called by their Valencian name, and where there is any possibility of confusion, the Spanish name is given afterwards.

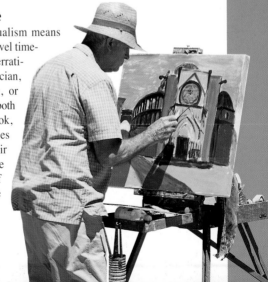

Left: El Micalet
Right: capturing the city's colour

1. THE CITY CENTRE, OLD AND NEW *(see map, p24)*

Explore the atmospheric old town, feast your eyes on the central market's food stalls and enjoy lunch nearby. In the afternoon, visit the city's stunning modern art museum and lush botanical garden.

Sitting at the heart of the old town, the **Plaça de la Mare de Déu** – also called the Plaza de la Virgen – is a harmonious patchwork of buildings and polished marble flagstones. Here you feel the city's pulse. Doves and pigeons flutter around a sensual fountain representing the city's river. Strolling couples, an historic weekly water court, weddings, skateboarders and fiestas fill it with life. Much of the city's history is focused on this square.

The Cathedral

On the square's eastern side sits the honey-coloured cathedral, **La Seu** (Apr–Oct Mon–Sat 10am–6.30pm, Sun 2–6.30pm; Nov–Mar Mon–Sat 10am–5.30pm, Sun closed 2–5pm; free) and, next door, the domed Basilica. Facing them, overlooking a small orange garden, is the oldest wing of the Palau de la Generalitat, where the city's town hall stood from the 16th to 19th centuries. It is still occupied by the regional government. Behind that is the 18th-century public library, built as a changing room for ceremonial occasions.

Even on a brief visit, do not miss the circular walk around La Seu's walls. A clockwise stroll starting at the Gothic Porta dels Apòstols, topped by a splendid rose window, takes you past a street shrine and tiled fresco, then under gargoyles to the splendid Romanesque Porta del Almoína. Walking on round under the archbishop's footbridge that spans Car-

Above: Plaça de la Mare de Déu. **Left:** taking a break in the square. **Right:** nuns at the cathedral

rer Barchella you reach the cathedral's exuberant three-tiered baroque Porta dels Ferros. Its curious dimensions were tailored to open on to a narrow street.

Just inside is the entrance to the cathedral's 14th-century belltower, **El Micalet** (Little Michael; Apr–Oct daily 10am–sunset; Nov–Mar 10am–1pm only; admission fee), affectionately nicknamed after its 11,000-kg (24,255-lb) rooftop bell. Delicate stonework, like a lacy shawl, decorates the top of the tower. If you climb the 207 steep spiral steps you will be rewarded by splendid 360-degree rooftop views over the cathedral's eight small blue teapot domes and alabaster-windowed lantern to the distant port. Time your climb well and you will catch Little Michael booming out the hour.

The Holy Grail

Three decades of restoration have returned the cathedral's interior to its original Gothic and Renaissance style. The most exciting recent discovery is on the ceiling – a series of late 15th-century Italian frescoes, luminous after 300 years hidden behind baroque plasterwork. Restoration has stabilised their condition and brought out their vibrancy. Another highlight is the florid **Capella del Sant Calze**, or Chapel of the Holy Grail, where an intricate carved altarpiece frames a gilt cup claimed to be the Holy Grail. 'It is a disappointing object which might have come from Tiffany's,' wrote V.S. Pritchett in *The Spanish Temper*. But the carved ceiling and altarpiece are stunning.

Nearby, two intriguing Goya paintings hang in the **Capella dels Borja**, the chapel of the infamous Valencia-born Borgia family. It leads to the small cathedral **Museum** (Mon–Fri 10am–6.30pm, Sat 10am–5.30pm, Sun 2–5.30pm; closed on Sun Nov–Mar 2–5pm; admission fee), where you can get a close-up view of the original statues from the Porta dels Apóstols plus the cathedral's most valuable early paintings and sculptures. The whole cathedral is very much a place of worship rather than a museum, and early birds can catch sung mass at 9am. Behind the main altar pregnant women pause to pray at the 15th-century alabaster Virgen del Coro who blesses childbirth.

A circular 20-minute walk in the cathedral quarter rounds up other sights that allow you to travel in time. Behind the Romanesque Porta del Almoína lies **L'Almoína**, once the hub of the Roman, Visigothic and Muslim city, now transformed into a plaza designed around its rich archaeological remains. Crossing it you arrive at **L'Almodí** (L'Almudín; Tues–Sat 10am–2pm, 4.30–8.30pm, Sun 10am–3pm; free; enter from Plaça Sant Lluís Bertran), a 15th-century granary, once fortified and now used as an exhibition space. Its 18th-century frescoes of the wheat harvest sit above painted markers that showed the stored grain's level.

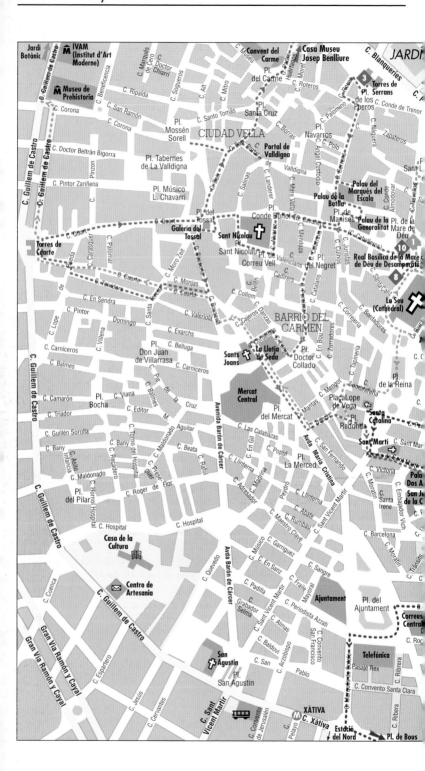

Cutting down Salvador, you reach Plaça Sant Llorenç, which is dominated by the austere façade of Les Corts, or regional parliament. It had many former lives: as a grammar school, the Borgias' palace and a thread factory.

From here it is a short walk up Navellos to the Plaça de la Mare de Déu. You can dip briefly into the **Real Basílica de la Mare de Déu de Desamparats** (daily 7am–2pm, 4.30–9pm; free), named after its tiny, richly jewelled 15th-century virgin, Our Lady of the Forsaken, who floats on puffy silver clouds above the altar. Her nodding head has given her the nickname *La Geperudeta*, or little hunchback. Such is the devotion to her that she draws a full house of young and old for 10 masses throughout the day.

El Mercat, the raffish neighbouring market quarter, is less graceful but much livelier than the quiet streets surrounding the cathedral. The quickest route there (10 minutes' walk) is via Plaça de la Reina and Sombrerería, a short pedestrianised alley where you might like to pause at one of two cafés, either Santa Catalina or El Siglo. Both of them make delicious *orxata (horchata)* – cold tiger-nut milk. A winter alternative is a cup of hot chocolate so thick that a spoon can stand up in it.

city itineraries

At the end of Sombrerería you will come to Plaça Lope de Vega. Off to the left is the entrance to the **Plaça Redonda**, an endearing miniature open-air market locally nicknamed El Clot (The Hole). Guard your wallet or purse and enjoy the old-fashioned haberdashery, handbag and ceramics stalls and shops. On Sundays, the liveliest day, song-bird traders fill the plaza.

The Silk Exchange

From here it is a stone's throw up C. Trench to the Plaça del Mercat, once the old town's main square. Here you will find the city's architectural gem, **La Llotja de Seda** (Silk Exchange; Tues–Sat 10am–2pm, 4.30–8.30pm, Sun 10am–3pm; free). Pere Comte, a local stonemason, designed the building at the end of the 16th century as the business city's general trading centre. Conceived then as a cathedral to trade, it is still breathtaking. In the main hall, ribbed vaulting sprouts from slender, twisted columns that soar, like palm trees, 18m (59ft) above the patterned floor. In the lovely patio garden, stairs lead to the small Consulat de Mar, where a court – which could send traders to prison in the tower upstairs – sat. It has a stunningly crafted 15th-century carved wooden ceiling and a spiral stone staircase, a major engineering feat for its time, as it has no central vertical support.

Across the road you will see the sculpted 18th-century façade of the Iglesia de los Santos Joans and, to its left, the city's splendid art nouveau food market. The **Mercat Central** (Mon–Sat 7am–2.30pm; free), a hive of activity, houses 959 food stalls under two wrought-iron-and-stained-glass domes with painted tiled friezes depicting fruit and flowers. Colourful street stalls at the front sell paella pans, earthenware wine jugs and a range of tapas that will make your mouth water. Inside, everything is beautifully displayed: local specialities include baked pumpkins and a dozen types of salted and dried fish. Fresh fish stalls are set aside in their own hall.

Above: the Mercat Central. **Above right:** the Botanical Garden
Right: the main hall of La Llotja

Next door to the market you can enjoy lunch at the Bar de la Llotja (Palafox 1, tel: 96 351 20 77), a small, friendly restaurant, whose great set menus always include paella. It serves take-away food to stallholders from early morning.

In the afternoon you can visit two old-town sights that reveal different sides of the city's character. Just a 20-minute walk – or a five-minute taxi-ride away – via Bossería, Cuarte and Guillem de Castro – is the city's modern art gallery, **IVAM** (Institut Valencià d'Art Moderne; Tues–Sun 10am–8pm; admission fee except Sun and public holidays). Housed in a sleek modern block opened in 1989, it was Spain's first modern art museum and it remains one of the most respected. The permanent collection, focused on the interplay between 20th-century sculpture and painting, fills two floors. Excellent shows by international artists fill the other three main spaces, while a basement gallery incorporates a large chunk of the 11th-century Muslim city wall. A small café downstairs makes a good spot to lounge in the sun.

Botanical Garden

Fifteen minutes' walk away at Quart 80 is the **Jardí Botànic** (daily Mar–Nov 10am–7pm, until later in summer; Dec–Feb until 6pm; admission fee), Spain's oldest botanical garden, established in the 16th century. Replanted here in 1803, and recently restored to glory, the garden is a refuge from the city's noise and traffic. Among the 3,000 species growing are exotic and semi-tropical trees that flourish in the humid climate. They include a huge yucca, a 30-trunk palm (La Carasa) and a 34-m (112-ft) high pecan tree. There are also giant succulents, native flora, medicinal plants and a wild area. There's an excellent museum shop, too.

For dinner you can take your pick between two restaurants that give a taste of modern Mediterranean cuisine. La Sucursal (Guillem de Castro 118, tel: 96 374 66 65), on the first floor of IVAM, has been earning rave reviews for its avant-garde gourmet cooking. If you prefer something less pricy, La Lola (Pujada del Toledà 8, tel: 96 391 80 45), right next to the cathedral, is good for a fun night out. At midnight the modern restaurant becomes a bar (with DJs), where you can sip cocktails into the early hours.

2. DOWN THE RIVER TURIA *(see map, p30)*

A walk through the modern gardens planted in the Turia's riverbed leads you from the Museum of Fine Arts to the bold City of Arts and Sciences. Along the same route you will find the child-friendly Natural History Museum and play areas. Finally, visit the stunning aquarium.

The gardens and parks planted in the Turia's riverbed since the 1980s are still maturing, but they already make a wonderful green corridor curving around the old town's northern edge. It provides a fine walking route between two of the city's major cultural attractions: the Museu de Belles Artes (Museum of Fine Arts) and the futuristic Ciutat de les Arts i de les Ciències (City of Arts and Sciences). Along the 2.5-km (1½-mile) walk are 11 bridges, ranging from medieval to hi-tech, a post-modern park, where dozens of waterspouts bubble into tiled waterways, small lakes, children's play areas and picnicking spots. Steps climbing out of the riverbed at various points offer the chance to break the walk, or to pick it up half-way through.

Museum of Fine Arts

The **Museu de Belles Artes** (Tues–Sun 10am–8pm; free; allow 1½ hours) at Sant Pius V 9, just west of Pont de la Trinitat on the river's north bank, can be picked out by its azure teapot dome. Once a seminary, it was slickly refurbished in the 1990s to house the city's collection of Old Masters. The ground-floor galleries, dedicated to Valencian Gothic and Renaissance art, show a series of magnificent altarpieces from churches and convents

Above: the City of Arts and Sciences by night
Left: Old Master in the Museum of Fine Arts

dissolved by the state in 1837. Upstairs is more of a mixed bag. The high points are Velázquez's famous self-portrait and a trio of sharply observed Goya portraits. Back downstairs, do not miss the Patio de Vich, a transplanted Renaissance courtyard.

Children may prefer the neighbouring **Museu de Ciències Naturals** (Tues–Sat 9.30am–2pm, 4.30–8pm, Sun 10am–8pm; admission fee). This excellent little natural history museum inside the Jardins del Reial opened in 1902, but it has been given a recent facelift with lots of audio-visual exhibits, all with English-language options. One section explains the province's main ecosystems, including that of the nearby Albufera. Downstairs is the museum's star – the skeleton of a giant Megatherium. Outside is a pleasant café, where you can soak up the sun while you enjoy tapas and ice cream.

Five minutes' walk back up the north bank a stairway next to the 16th-century **Pont dels Serrans** leads down to the riverbed. In the first stretch of the walk east are purple-flowering jacaranda trees, palms and Mediterranean pines, and good views of the old town. The first bridge you walk under is Pont de la Trinitat, the city's oldest, dating back to 1402 and built from stout stone blocks designed to resist the full flow of the winter river. After that, oleanders, wild pepper and ficus trees are planted on grassy banks running down to two more bridges. These are a fabulous contrast: first the 16th-century Pont Reial and then Valencia-born Santiago Calatrava's streamlined 1990s bridge nicknamed **La Peineta** (The Hair Comb; *see page 76*). It sits above his hangar-like Alameda metro station, which glitters with *trencadís* – the broken tile mosaics first used by Gaudí.

After two more bridges – the first is the flowery Pont de Flores – you enter post-modern gardens, where dozens of waterspouts, orange trees and a formal colonnade frame a small lake below the city's concert hall, the **Palau de la Música**. Its 1980s glass-roofed design was inspired by London's Crystal Palace and the city's central market.

Lunch Break

The Palau is a good place to stop for lunch. Its light-filled lunchtime café serving paellas and set lunches is open from 1.30pm (tel: 96 337 20 21), or you can leave the riverbed for a good-value gourmet lunch at Michelin-starred Alejandro (Amadeo de Saboya 15, tel: 96 393 40 46), an unfussy restaurant attracting a young crowd, 10 minutes' walk away.

From the Palau de la Música it is another half-hour's walk down to the City of Arts and Sciences. If you have young children with you, they may like to stop off at the **Parc de Gulliver** (daily 10am–8pm; free). Here, a vast, sprawling figure of Gulliver incorporates various activities in an imaginative play area.

Above: lush palms at the City of Arts and Sciences

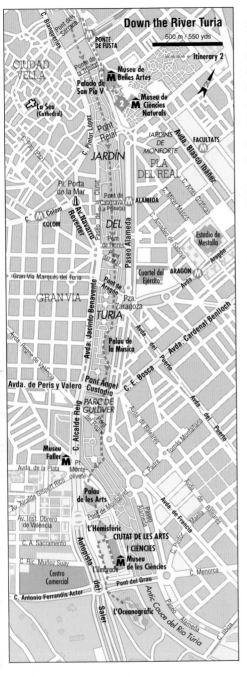

By now you will have caught a first glimpse of the Ciutat's most spectacular building: the 75-m (246-ft) high **Palau de les Arts**, designed by Calatrava. Its mass of curving forms – sometimes suggesting a fish, at other moments an armadillo – are highlighted by a glittering white cladding of *trencadís*. Opened in 2005, it is a world-class arts venue.

Paths lead from the Palau under Montolivet bridge to a rectangular lake framed by the city's main buildings. The largest one, a curving skeletal structure, houses an interactive science museum, the **Museu de Les Ciències Príncep Felip**. Next to it, in the centre of the lake, a small, eye-shaped pod, **L'Hemisfèric**, covers a planetarium-cum-IMAX cinema. On the far side of the lake stands **L'Umbracle**, a tall, arched and shaded walkway edged by funnel-like openings tiled with broken ceramics. L'Umbracle harbours an extraordinary garden, featuring palms, orange trees, carpets of flowers and over 450 climbers.

You may like simply to enjoy the architecture or you can visit the **Museu de les Ciències** (daily 10am–7pm; July–Sept until 9pm; admission fee). Three floors of interactive displays and modules explore themes from nature and the history of human life. Children's highlights include the sports area and the Space Academy. L'Hemisfèric's IMAX cinema (11am–9pm; programme at the ticket office; admission fee), has multilingual and children's sessions. But the outstanding visit here is the aquarium, **L'Oceanogràfic** (Jan–mid-June, mid-Sept–Dec daily 10am–6pm; mid-June–July, early Sept 10am–8pm; Aug 10am–midnight; admis-

Right: Plaça de la Mare de Déu, in the Barri del Carme

sion fee). This is the building's final complex, located beyond the Pont del Grau and designed by Spanish architect Félix Candelas. Tropical and temperate fish that swim all around you in its spectacular 70-m (230-ft) walk-through acrylic tunnel *(see page 89)*. Another highlight is the Arctic area, where beluga whales swim in icy water. You need at least two hours to enjoy everything, especially if you want to see the 20-minute open-air dolphin show.

When hunger overtakes you, there are six different eating areas, ranging from a luxury floating underwater restaurant to an ice-cream parlour.

If you would prefer an evening out, there are half a dozen good restaurants just a short taxi drive away. You could book a table at Albacar (Sorní 35, tel: 96 395 10 05), which offers excellent modern Mediterranean cooking based on Tito Albacar's personal style; or at El Ángel Azul (Conde de Altea 33, tel: 96 374 56 56), a good-value alternative. Both have modern, stylish but informal dining rooms.

3. EL BARRI DEL CARME *(see map, p24)*

The medieval streets of El Carme – or El Carmen – are studded with urban palaces, churches, small museums and countless eye-catching architectural details. After exploring its web of streets and alleys on foot, you can sample a local lunch at a classic tavern.

For centuries the elegant, fortified **Torres de Serrans** (Tues–Sat 10am–2pm, 4.30–8.30pm, Sun 10am–3pm only; free) formed Valencia's main gateway, opening on to the road north to Barcelona. From 1586 to 1892 the towers were also used as a prison for nobility and so they escaped demolition when the rest of the walls were pulled down in 1865. Today they make a splendid entrance to the Barri del Carme's medieval streets. The gateway keeps its original wooden door, fabulous gargoyles and a reproduction

of the bell used to announce the gate's night-time closing. At the back the towers were left open so that they could not be used as a base for attacking the town.

Straight ahead lies **Carrer Serrans** (Calle Serrano), named after Aragonese sierra warriors who were given houses here following the Christian reconquest. The road marks the eastern boundary between El Carme and the cathedral quarter. Before heading down it, you can make a first stop at the **Museu de Corpus Christi** (Tues–Sat 10am–2pm, 4.30–8.30pm, Sun 10am–3pm; admission fee) at Roteros 8, where processional carts and giant figures that form the Corpus Christi procession are kept in a restored medieval building. The oldest of the richly decorated *roques*, or carts, made in 1511, sprouts a family of black and red devils. Round the corner from the museum stands the original timbered Casa de les Roques, a glorified tall-doored garage where the carts were kept until recently.

Craftsmen's Quarter

Returning to Serrans via Roteros you will pass Montaner, a family bakery, at No 5, where a chunk of the city's 11th-century wall is embedded in the shop, and the glass counters are stacked with home-made cakes and biscuits. Turning right on to Serrans you will begin to notice the quarter's intriguing architectural details: old street lamps, tiled wrought-iron balconies, recycled stone columns and old glazed ceramic tiles, for example.

Once this was an area of craft workshops, whose owners lived above. Most closed in the 1990s, although one string-maker is left (at No 10). On the right, one of the Civil War air-raid shelters, built in 1936 and marked 'Refugio' in art deco lettering, awaits restoration. At the end of the street, diving down Carrer Samaniego – a quiet alley to the left – you will find a splendid overhanging balcony at the back of the **Palau de la Batlia**. Made of wrought iron and glazed tiles, it measures 10m (33ft).

Just beyond is **Plaça de Manises**, a tight rectangular plaza surrounding an elegant sloping parterre. When Valencia was a kingdom, this was the hub of government life. The Palau de la Batlia, or residence of the bailiff who administered the Spanish crown's assets, is now home to the provincial government. During working hours you can peek through a glass door to see the splendid patio. Next door, the 16th-century **Palau del Marqués del Escala** (Tues–Sat 11am–2pm, 5–8pm, Sun 10am–2pm; free) has a long-term exhibition on the cathedral's recently discovered Renaissance frescoes, and visitors can also admire the splendid 18th-century staircase. On the opposite side of the plaza is the **Palau de la Generalitat**, the seat of the regional government, Gothic in origin but only completed in the 20th century. It is open to the public only by special arrangement.

Noble Mansions

On the southern side of the square runs **Carrer Cavallers** (Calle Caballeros in Castilian) – literally Knights' Street, the city's main thoroughfare from Roman times until well into the 19th century. The urban palaces that line the street, with tall, carved wooden doors opening onto carriage courtyards, were built between the 15th and 19th centuries by aristocratic Valencian, Aragonese and Catalan families. Most of the palaces have found new owners and new uses, but they keep the names of the families who built them. The 14th-century Palau de Mercader, for example, at No 23, is now occupied by the region's main agricultural cooperative. During working hours you can walk into its double patio and get a good idea of the design.

If you feel like a coffee or a break, Café Cavallers, at No 25, is a good choice. Just beyond, on the far side of the Teatre Talia, Carrer Álvarez leads to **Plaça de Correu Vell**, a lovely tranquil square named after the city's first post office. The neighbouring square to the right is named after its church, **Sant Nicolau** (Sat 9.30am–1pm, 6.30–8pm, Sun 10am–1pm), where the knightly residents once prayed. Legend has it that if you light a candle in a side-chapel here on three consecutive Mondays, your request will be granted – but only if you keep silent as you travel to the church. On these 'Lunes de Sant Nicolau', queues wind round the block. The church is worth seeing anyway for its sumptuous, if faded, baroque frescoes, retablos by Joan de Joanes and colourful tiling.

Cavallers ends at **Plaça del Tossal**, a star-like crossroads with half a dozen cafés. Underneath is the **Galería del Tossal** (Tues–Sat 10am–2pm, 5–8pm, Sun 10am–2pm; admission fee), a small walk-through gallery built around another chunk of the Muslim wall and a square 12th-century tower. On one corner stands the Café

eft: the view from Torres de Serrans
bove: tiled street plaque. **Right:** door knocker in Carrer Cavallers

Bar Pilar (noon–midnight), a famous tapas bar specialising in *clóchinas* – mussels with paprika. Anything you order here is delicious.

This first part of the walk will take about 1½ hours. You can extend it via a short loop through the old wool- and silk-weavers' quarter to the **Torres de Cuarte** (or Quart), the other city gateway. Following Bossería and then cutting through to Guillem de Castro you will find narrow streets with evocative names such as Cardá and Teixidors – literally Comb and Weavers. The Torres de Cuarte, framing a chunky 15th-century stone gateway, are pleasantly unrestored. Pigeons nest in the 19th-century cannon-ball holes that were left as a reminder of the heroic uprising against the French in 1808.

Nightlife Area

The second half of the route, taking about an hour, runs north along **Carrer Baix** (Calle Baja) towards the river. This is the most tumble-down part of the quarter, and residents have long been campaigning for its restoration. After the reconquest this was the site of the *morería*, a walled area where Muslims lived among boggy market gardens. After their expulsion, it became a nightlife area. Inns operated beside a cockfighting theatre, and just to the north was one of Europe's largest brothel quarters, regulated by the town hall. Today, the area has a buzzing nightlife, but without the brothels.

After passing a small 1930s market, Mossén Sorell, off to the left, the next narrow street to the right (unsigned), opposite an old-people's residence, leads to one of the city's most unusual treasures, the **Portal de Valldigna**. This 15th-century archway, once framing a wooden door, was built over the entrance from the *morería* into the main town. A copy of a Gothic canvas hanging under the eaves shows Jaime I and the abbot of Santes Creus, who built Valldigna monastery on land given by the crown. Just before it, at No 15, a plaque marks the site of Spain's first printers, set up here in 1474.

Walking north up Carrer Baix brings you out on to the Plaça del Carme. A stone's throw to the left, on the far side of the church, stands the **Convent**

del Carme (Tues–Sun 10am–8pm; free), originally a closed convent, hence its high, windowless walls. In 1836 it became the city's art school, but since the 1990s it has been used as an exhibition space. Currently it houses the pick of the Fine Arts Museum's 19th- to 20th-century paintings and sculpture. You will find work by two of Valencia's most appealing artists, painter Joaquín Sorolla and sculptor Mariano Benlliure. Even if you do not want to see the collection, it is well worth dodging in here to admire the two patios, one Gothic and the other Renaissance.

A Bourgeois Home

Located close by, on riverside Blanqueries, where the tanners once worked, is another small museum, the **Casa-Museu Josep Benlliure** (Tues–Sat 10am–2pm, 4.30–8.30pm, Sun 10am–3pm; free). Less well known than his brother Mariano,

Josep Benlliure was a respected painter. More than 150 of his works and 200 oils by his gifted son Peppino, who died aged 32, are shown here, but the real charm of the museum, walled garden and studio is its evocation of a 19th-century home.

There are literally dozens of good places to eat in El Carmen. The classic choice is Ca'n Bermell (Sant Tomás 18, tel: 96 391 02 88), located close to Mossèn Sorell, where you can sample genuine Valencian cooking made with quality produce. If you only want a light meal there, it also has a bar, where you can graze on tapas.

4. THE DECORATIVE NEW TOWN *(see map, pp18–19)*

A circular route takes you around the spacious 18th- and 19th-century streets of the southern walled town. Here the city's taste for exuberant ornament is stamped on stunning baroque, rococo and art nouveau architecture. The decorative flair that still makes Valencian design distinctive is on display in elegant shop windows.

Plaça Alfons El Magnànim lies close to the central eastern point of the old city's walls. Centennial magnolia trees throw pools of shade here. This is a good departure point for a circular walk around the spacious 18th- and 19th-century streets that grew around orchards and vegetable

eft: Portal de Valldigna
op and above: bar and street scene in the Barri del Carme

gardens in the southern half of the walled town. Head off down Carrer Pau (Calle Paz), an elegant 19th-century street where you can window-shop for local perfumes or designer furniture.

The Ceramics Museum

Half-way along Carrer Pau, turn left down Poeta Querol to the **Palau de Dos Aigües** (Palace of Two Waters), unmissable for its swirling, heavily sculpted alabaster doorway and ornate plasterwork balconies. This exuberant façade, clad in grey and gold marble, is considered the high point of Spanish rococo architecture. Just next to the palace is a hotel with a café terrace that provides an ideal spot to contemplate the façade. Designed in the late 18th century by Valencian painter Hipólito Rovira and sculptor Ignacio Vergara, it pays homage to their patron's title – the Marquis of Two Waters. On either side of the door, crouching, muscle-bound Herculean figures hold jars of cascading water, representing the rivers Turia and Xúcar. Around them, other details, such as a crocodile, snake, palm tree and fruits, lend an air of exotic fantasy.

Today the palace houses the **Museu Nacional de Ceràmica i Arts Suntuaries González Martí** (Tues–Sat 10am–2pm, 4–8pm, Sun 10am–2pm; admission fee, except Sat pm and Sun am). There are two separate areas to visit. One is the first-floor palace, done out in French Empire style. The second is the excellent ceramics museum on the top floor. Together they take about 1½ hours to visit. A highlight of the ornate first-floor apartments is the Marquis' bedroom with an original marble bath and ceiling paintings. However, in general, the interior lacks the façade's magical originality.

The museum upstairs grew out of the private collection of the director of the Manises Ceramics School, hence the observant eye behind nearly 5,000 pieces laid out in 13 galleries. The scope here is fabulous. Valencia's styles, exported around the world at different times, are set against a wider backdrop sweeping from Classical Greece through the centuries of Muslim rule

Above: detail of the Palau de Dos Aigües
Right: tiled kitchen, Museu Nacional de Ceràmica

to recent times. The influence of Islamic taste on Valencian ceramics – for example, Manisa's famous shiny medieval lusterware – is remarkable. Among the many highlights are the ceramics decorated by Picasso and the recreated Valencian kitchen tiled with a collection of hand-painted 17th- to 19th-century tiles depicting vignettes of kitchen life.

Medieval Church

Continuing down Poeta Querol, you will pass the fat, twisted columns of **San Juan de la Cruz** (open for mass Sat 7.30pm, Sun 12.30pm and 8pm) on the right-hand side. One of the city's earliest medieval churches, built over a mosque, it has a dazzling rococo interior painted by Hipólito Rovira and is worth seeing if you can catch the limited opening hours.

When you reach Carrer Barques (Calle Barcas), cross over and take the next right, Correu. It brings you out on the Plaça del Ajuntament opposite the town hall, originally a girl's school, later crowned by twin copper-roofed towers. Facing it and designed to match is **Correus Central** (Mon–Fri 8.30am–8.30pm, Sat 8.30am–2pm), the post-office that was opened by King Alfonso XIII in 1922. Do not miss its stained-glass dome inside.

Outside, the fragrant kiosks of a small flower market run around the edge of the square to Marqués de Sotelo, which takes you to the site of the old city walls, where the wide streets of Xàtiva and Colom (or Colón) run today. Opposite sits a palatial, fairy-tale cream façade centred on a clock tower presided over by an eagle – in reality the central railway station, **Estació del Nord** (daily 5.15am–12.30am). Its fine details include garlands and wreaths of orange blossom, fruit, roses and even cabbage leaves. Inside, the lobby is also fabulously decorated with cream and pink ceramic mosaics, columns topped by sculpted ceramic fruit and flowers, brass globe lanterns and wall mosaics.

The Bull Ring

The station is one of a trio of grandiose civic structures built in this area just after the walls were pulled down. Next door is the large red-brick bull-ring, **Plaça de Bous** (Plaza de Toros; Tues–Fri 10am–8pm). Opened in 1859, it was designed as a huge amphitheatre evoking Rome's Coliseum, with a capacity for 17,000. Nowadays it is used for rock concerts and cir-

cuses as well as spring and summer bullfights *(corridas)*. Those who are intrigued by the *fiesta nacional*, as bullfighting is called, can visit the ring and its bull-pen, chapel, surgery and presidential box. Round the back, at No 10 in the scruffy, covered Pasaje Dr Serra, is the small **Museu Taurí** (Tues–Sun 10am–8pm), Spain's first bullfighting museum, founded in 1929. It gives a good feel of *corrida* culture, showcasing Valencian bullfighting heroes, their glittery embroidered suits, posters and a set of Goya's famous series of bullfighting prints. A brief detour from here leads to another fantasy building, Miami style, at Carrer Castello 20.

Shopping Centre

A short walk via Colom, Russafa and Cirilo Amorós, all busy fashionable shopping streets, to the left, leads you to the cathedral-like **Mercat de Colom**

(Mon–Sat 7am–1.30am). Designed as a food market at the turn of the 20th century, when the local art nouveau movement – *modernisme* – was in full swing, its lofty red-brick shell, decorated with ceramics, stained glass and sculpted fruit, is now restored as an upmarket shopping centre.

If you feel like completing the full circular walk, continue down Cirilo Amarós past wonderfully elegant shops and 19th-century façades. At No 22 the designs of Francisco Montesinos, the city's best-known fashion designer, reflect Valencia's love of extravagance. Turning left down Jorge Juan to return to Colom, you will pass another art deco building, the Casa de los Dragones, at the junction with Sorní. You are in the heart of gourmet restaurant land here. One appropriate choice would be Gargantúa (Navarro Reverter 18, tel: 96 334 68 49), which serves good Mediterranean food and wine in an attractive turn-of-the-20th-century dining room.

Top: Plaça de Bous – the bullring
Above: Mercat de Colom. **Right:** Malva Rosa beach

5. MALVA ROSA: PAELLA AT THE BEACH
(see map, p42)

The tram to breezy seaside Malva Rosa takes you to a broad beach boulevard. On it stands novelist Vicente Blasco Ibáñez's summer home, now a museum. After a walk or swim you can have lunch or dinner by the long sandy beach.

The tram from the city centre (marked for Dr Lluch) can be picked up close to the river from Pont de Fusta. The old railway station building is now a police station, and the new open-air platform lies behind it. Machines issue flat-rate tickets. The tram is a modern affair, running quietly past a pleasantly jumbled urban landscape – you will see 1960s apartment blocks, palm trees and the Politécnica's high-rise faculties, which have eaten into the last inner-city patch of market gardens.

Get off at Eugenia Viñes – the ninth stop – next to low houses with colourful tiled façades. These 19th- and early 20th-century fishermen's homes, small shops and hostels, which replaced thatched *barracas*, have given the seaside quarter its own architectural style – a low-budget, characterful art nouveau.

Sandy Shore

Cross the road to reach Malva Rosa's wide seafront boulevard and the beach, which grew into a broad expanse of white sand after 1792, when the port's first permanent wall was built and tides began to deposit sand here. As the beach became increasingly welcoming, so city families arrived in growing numbers. Some rented fishermen's homes, while wealthier families had their own houses built.

Turning north you pass an early 20th-century hospital and sanatorium and then spacious residences built by the bourgoisie in the late 19th and early 20th centuries. You may love or hate the eccentric designs of these summer homes, but there's no denying that they have personality.

On the east side, next to the beach, there are kiosk bars where you can stop to watch the world go by. In summer there is also an improvised street market that sells everything from candles to shoes.

Continuing north, a 10-minute walk along the broad strip of fine white sand leads to the end of the boulevard and a large, green 19th-century villa. This was the house of Valencian novelist Vicente Blasco Ibáñez (1867–1928), best known outside Spain for his 1916 novel *The Four Horsemen of the Apocalypse*, about World War I. On home ground he is better remembered for his fiery Republican politics and early novels based on late 19th-century Valencia. One of these, *Flor de Mayo* (1895), set in the fishing quarter, captures the life of the people who lived here. Another summer resident – a contemporary and friend of Blasco Ibáñez – was Joaquín Sorolla (1863–1923), Spain's most famous Impressionist artist, who immortalised Malva Rosa beach in his paintings.

At the end of his life Blasco Ibáñez went into voluntary political exile in France. The family's summer home was left abandoned and falling into

ruins until the 1990s, when the city authorities bought it and rebuilt it as a museum and study centre. Today, the **Casa-Museu Blasco Ibáñez** (Isabel de Villena s/n; Tues–Sat 10am–2pm, 4.30–8.30pm, Sun 10am–3pm; admission fee) has been restored to its original design, with caryatids supporting the first-floor porch, and a large garden with palm trees. The museum collection, split between two floors, includes first editions of novels in various languages, copies of *El Pueblo*, the anti-monarchical newspaper that the writer founded, furniture, family paintings and photographs. It gives an interesting impression of wealthy liberal Valencian life at the beginning of the 20th century.

Paella or Picnics

After seeing the house you can enjoy a leisurely lunch or dinner. There are plenty of choices. Next door to the museum is La Carmela (Isabel de Villena 155, tel: 96 371 00 73), which has been serving paellas and seafood since the 1920s. Its specialities, such as the home-cured anchovies, are excellent. A cheaper alternative, situated right on the beach, is La Herradura (Passeig Marítim de Valencia 2, tel: 96 371 59 81); or Casa Navarro (Passeig Marítim de la Alboraia s/n, tel: 96 372 00 27), 10 minutes' walk further north on Platja de Patacona.

Another option is to buy a picnic before leaving town (there are few shops on the seafront) and take it to the beach. On weekends, continue north across the Acequia de La Vera to find a quiet space on the sand.

To return to town, either catch the tram back to Pont de Fusta or, to see the port, take the No 19 bus from the boulevard. It will take you along the sea-front and past the docks, leaving you finally at the Plaça del Ajuntament.

Above: enjoying paella at the beach
Right: Casa-Museu Blasco Ibáñez

6. THE PORT QUARTER:
EL CABANYAL-CANYEMALAR *(see map, p42)*

El Cabanyal, once a seaside town, is now absorbed into the city but has kept its traditional maritime character. A short walk leads to the revamped dock harbour, small museums, a *bodega* bar and lively, popular fish restaurants. Every Thursday morning there is a large street market.

The quickest way to reach the port is to catch the No 19 bus from the Plaça del Ajuntament. Before it swings north to run along the seafront, it will leave you at the end of the avenue that leads down to El Grao, the docks. Here is a splendid cluster of art nouveau buildings and, just a few yards beyond the bus stop, a legendary old bar called Antigua Casa Calabuig (Avinguda del Port/Puerto 336), which serves great tapas from 6am to midnight.

The Revamped Docks

From here you will see **El Grao**, originally a portable wooden wharf, built in 1237 and transplanted from one spot to another as the river and tidal patterns changed. Vilanova del Grao, the small town that grew behind it, began to spread after the first fixed port wall was built in 1792 and a railway link to the city arrived, in 1852. A few decades later, as the export of oranges flourished, the red-brick Estació Marítim and Tinglado, an open-sided, wrought-iron hangar, were built. Both keep their eye-catching art nouveau details.

The docks were revamped for the 32nd America's Cup yacht race, held here in 2007. The Tinglado temporarily made way for the teams' hi-tech designer pavilions, which were open for public visits. The docks are also playing host to the 33rd America's Cup, in 2009.

In the meantime, the small boat that runs harbour trips is without a base, although its departure point can usually be spotted in the inner harbour. The 30-minute trip is a fun way to see the impressive spread of the industrial port (tel: 96 316 41 77 to ensure a ticket and for times).

Above: practising for the America's Cup in the port

A five-minute walk back up the Avinguda del Port (Avenida del Puerto) will take you to the Plaça Tribunal de los Aigües, a pretty square that leads to the **Museu de les Drassanes** (Tues–Sat 10am–2pm, 4.30–8.30pm, Sun 10am–3pm), also called Las Atarazanas, the city's splendid shipyard. Erected in the late 14th and early 15th centuries, its wooden roof spans the wide aisles where ships were built and goods warehoused until the 19th century. This was the city's largest building for a long time and is a good indication of the importance of medieval Valencia's maritime trade. The building houses both a naval museum (the Museo Marítimo Joaquín Saludes) and temporary exhibitions.

Holy Images and Rice

From the Drassanes it is a short walk around Carrer de Escalante to Francesc Cubells, where a large brick warehouse lies almost directly opposite on the other side of Carrer Rosario. Inside are two small museums. The **Casa-Museu Setmana Santa Marinera** (Tues–Sat 10am–2pm, 4.30–8.30pm, Sun 10am–3pm; admission fee) stores the religious Holy Week images, or *pasos*, that are processed by different church brotherhoods through the seaside quarters. Mainly modern, they range from kitschy, glamorous, doll-like Virgins to touchingly simple crucifixes that are carried down to the sands.

The second museum, next door, revives the original use of the building as a rice mill and warehouse. In the excellent **Museu de l'Arròs** (Tues–Sat 10am–2pm, 4.30–8.30pm, Sun 10am–3pm; admission fee) you will see the wooden 19th- and 20th-century machinery restored to use and run at half its normal working speed. A guided tour, in English, starts with a video and then takes you up and down the three floors of the mill, explaining how the rice was cleaned, husked, polished and stored.

Valencia's docklands also used to be home to countless *bodegas*, or wine cellars. The wine, brought down in barrels from the vineyards, was traded and stored here before shipping. One old *bodega*, now a tavern, survives just a short walk away, through the heart of Cabanyal-Canyemalar, the quarter that grew behind El Grao. After terrible fires in 1796 and 1875 its thatched fishermen's *barracas* were gradually rebuilt as low-level terraced houses with colourful tiled façades. This is one of the city's most appealing and popular neighbourhoods, urban yet with a traditional family feel. Keep going down Rosario until you reach the pretty **Plaça del Rosario**, complete with its restored theatre, church and fountain.

Above right: inside the rice museum. **Right:** Plaça del Rosario

You will find Bodegas Montaña at No 69 (tel: 96 367 23 14). Opened in the 1830s as two homes combined into a shop, a place of residence, an eatery and a *bodega*, it has become a gourmet sanctuary, famous for its choice of wines sold by the glass. There are also excellent tapas, based on simple ideas prepared with the very best ingredients, and served in a welcoming and relaxed atmosphere.

A little further down José Benlliure is Avinguda del Mediterrani. If you turn left here you come to El Cabanyal food market, around which a street market sprawls on Thursday mornings. Turning right, you walk straight down to Las Arenas beach. Once a wonderful old spa stood here. Badly damaged in the Civil War, it was auctioned off and has now been redeveloped as a luxury hotel. But keep going south beyond the hotel and you will rediscover Cabanyal's old-world, small-scale charms. A colourfully painted terrace of rice and fish restaurants backs on to the beach. The local custom is to ring ahead for a table and order the kind of rice you want in advance. Alternatively, you can book a table on the spot and then go for a walk or a quick swim while your dish is prepared. Everyone has their favourite, but two firm recommendations are La Rosa (Passeig Neptú 70, tel: 96 371 20 76), for fatter wallets, and Monkili (Passeig Neptú 52, tel: 96 371 00 39) for slimmer budgets.

7. JARDINS DE MONFORTE *(see map, p24)*

When you walk through the Jardins de Monforte's wrought-iron gates you enter perfectly preserved 19th-century gardens that close out the modern world. Thanks to their microclimate the gardens are in flower for most of the year. Located close by are the Jardins del Reial, where a royal palace once stood, and terrace cafés.

The walled **Jardins de Monforte** (daily 10.30am–sunset) sit on the north bank of the river, a stone's throw from the Pont Reial. Do not be misled by the uninspiring approach road, Carrer Monforte. Playful topiary, statues, a pond, a rose garden and shady old trees make this one of the Spanish Mediterranean's most beautiful gardens. They can be visited in half an hour, but you may like to linger longer.

When the Marqués de San Juan bought this land in 1860, palatial summer retreats were clustered between orchards and market gardens. By contrast, the Monforte pavilion is quite modest, while its gardens are lavish. Perhaps the Marqués, a businessman called Juan Bautista Romero who had recently been ennobled, preferred a low-key statement of wealth and power.

The gardens have survived intact thanks to the Marqués' family, who tended them for more than a century. In 1941 they were protected as a heritage garden and in the 1980s they were given to the town hall. In summer, early morning and dusk are good times to visit, for the subtlety of the light, and in winter one can soak up the sun at midday.

Gardens Formal and Informal

The entrance to the gardens is through the pavilion, where two marble lions guard the front gate. Walking through the hallway, where a staircase sweeps up to the first floor, you emerge on to a pebbled terrace with stairs, which lead up to the formal garden: a waist-high labyrinth of ingeniously trimmed hedges, Italian marble statues and a graceful fountain. The garden's second large section, separated by a tall myrtle arcade topped by geometric topiary, mixes formal and informal areas. A romantic bougan-villaea bower, loaded with purple flowers from early spring to late autumn, leads through to a large informal area of shady olive trees, palms, orange trees, gingkos and a huge magnolia. A fragrant rose garden encircles a tall bay tree. Beyond is a large oriental lily and bamboo pond, with vistas through beds of orange trees, and a woody hummock designed to be explored via a *trompe-l'oeil* winding path. Wherever you walk in this part of the garden, water splashes close by, from a spout, a fountain or a

Above: gate to the Jardins de Monforte

tap. In the back of the garden are sheets of colour where flowerbeds are replanted throughout the year.

If you would like to see a second garden, the **Jardins del Reial** (Royal Gardens; daily 8am–sunset) are a five-minute walk east along the river bank. You enter the park where the gardens around the first Muslim palace stood. Rubble marks the former royal palace of Jaime I, which was destroyed in 1810 to stop French troops using it as a base. Close by are shady palms and a modern sculpture of the Dama de Elx, Spain's most precious Iberian treasure. Further into the park are a large children's play zone, rose garden, *pétanque* pitch and a café.

Terrace with Tapas Views

Alternatively, the Passeig de L'Albereda (Paseo de la Alameda), a riverside boulevard by the Jardins de Monforte, has a fashionable terraced café for a drink or snack. Most characterful – and worth a special visit – is Kiosco la Pergola (Passeig de L'Albereda; summer 8am–11.30pm, but closed in Aug; winter 8am–sunset). You can sit in the sun and watch the cooks turn out wonderful tapas, such as grilled squid, to order.

8. MUSLIM VALENCIA *(see map, p24)*

The city's rich Muslim heritage includes a fascinating water culture. Every Thursday morning the Tribunal de les Aigües, which has been resolving farmers' water disputes since the 10th century, meets by the cathedral. Close by are the newly restored 14th-century Moorish public baths.

The **Tribunal de les Aigües,** founded around AD960 during the Cordoban caliphate, is one of Europe's oldest working courts. For more than a millennium it has been meeting every Thursday to settle water disputes between farmers. Its eight members, or *sindicos*, represent the eight main irrigation canals, or *acequias*, which channel water from the River Turia through the city's fertile market gardens. As the clock strikes noon, eight men in farmers'

Above: the Thursday Tribunal de les Aigües

black smocks file from the 18th-century Casa de Vestuaria led by the court's constable and take their seats in a circle outside the cathedral's Porta dels Apóstols. A warden calls to the public for complaints. If there is none, the court finishes in five minutes; if there is a dispute, the tribunal discusses the case, and any fine is imposed in *lliures valencianes*, the city's medieval currency. Valencian, the language of the farmland, is spoken. There is no paperwork, and there is no appeals system against its decisions.

For all the court's apparent simplicity, it works so well that few of its practices have changed. Ownership of the river water for irrigation purposes is communal, and each farmer's rights are fixed by the size of their land and the rules of the *acequia* to which they belong. Farmers who infringe the rules must answer to the tribunal. The proceedings are carried out in public to ensure transparency. The members, farmers themselves, are elected every two years, and the presidency shifts between the southern and northern channels to ensure that they never judge cases on their own territory.

Since a reservoir was built to supplement summer water shortfalls, there have been few disputes. However, the court remains an entirely genuine institution. If you would like to see it, go to the Porta dels Apóstols at least 20 minutes beforehand, as it always attracts a big crowd, and it is hard to get a good view.

Medieval Bathhouse

Muslim culture has given Valencia many living traditions, such as ceramics, citrus groves and rice cookery. However, little of its architecture survives. The best-preserved example is a 14th-century public bathhouse, 10 minutes' walk from the cathedral, the **Banys de L'Almirall** (Baños del Almirante; Tues–Sat 10am–2pm, 6–8pm, Sun 10am–2pm only; the door opens for vis-

its every 30 minutes; free), in a street of the same name. Today, after six centuries of public use and 16 years of restoration, they are open for visits. A short multilingual film explains the history of the baths. Built in 1313 for Christian use and modelled on earlier Islamic steam baths, they were probably built by workmen from the city's *morería*, the Muslim quarter. A half-hour guided visit takes in the changing room *(maslah)*, hot steam room *(bayt al-rajma)*, warm room *(bayt al-wastanir)* and cold room *(bayt al-barid)*. Star-shaped skylights trapped the sun's warmth, and water from the city-centre *acequia* was heated in a giant copper cauldron over a wood fire, then piped under the floors. The heat levels and original furniture have been recreated too.

Left: Banys de L'Almirall

The Arab Wall

Elsewhere you can see fragments of the 11th- to 12th-century Arab wall, built when Valencia was an independent *taifa* state. Its watchtowers were at first semicircular and later square. The wall was built over the watercourse of the oxbow river within which the city grew, and the best fragments survive in the Barri del Carme. Some have been restored – for example the 12th-century square tower revealed under Galería del Tossal *(see page 33)* and the long chunk within IVAM, the modern art museum *(see page 27)*. Other fragments are soon to be linked by a walking route. In the meantime it is worth seeking out the most spectacular – the Torre del Àngel, a tall, semi-circular 11th-century tower, which rears up above Carrer de la Cruz.

9. A TRIO OF OLD TOWN CHURCHES
(see map, p24)

The old town's churches offer a splendid spread of architectural styles. San Juan del Hospital contains Romanesque frescoes and Santa Catalina is Gothic, with a graceful baroque belltower. The Colegio del Patriarca has richly coloured baroque frescoes, an alligator and a fine painting collection. All three are open for visits every day of the week.

San Juan del Hospital (Mon–Fri 7–8am, 9.30am–1.30pm, 5–9pm; Sat 9.30am–1.30pm, 5–9pm; Sun 11am–2pm, 5–9pm; small admission fee) at Trinquet de Cavallers 5, is said to be the city's oldest church. In many ways it is a miracle that it has survived. The oldest parts date back to 1238, when the Order of St John of the Hospitallers was given land by Jaime I in thanks for their help in conquering the city. They built a simple chapel and hospital, then rebuilt a larger church. Damaged in the 17th century and abandoned in the 1830s, and burned during the Civil War, it was saved

Above: family fun

city itineraries

by local residents and declared a national monument in 1943. Standing off one of the old town's loveliest streets, St John's is now a museum as well as a church. Both are owned by the Opus Dei. A guide sheet details features otherwise easy to miss. The collage of architectural styles ranges from Muslim brick vaulting to a heavily decorated baroque chapel. Close to the altar, on the left-hand side, the **Capilla de San Miguel Arcangel** is decorated with rich 13th-century Romanesque frescoes found a few years ago under a thick layer of whitewash. They show the clear influence of Islamic geometric design. Towards the back, almost opposite the main doorway, sits Our Lady of the Students, a 12th-century statue. As you leave through the patio you will see the original arches of the 13th-century hospital outlined on the opposite wall.

Santa Catalina

Turning right out of the church on to Trinquet and crossing over Plaça Sant Vicent Ferrer, you come to a junction with Carrer Pau (Calle Paz). At its eastern end, the street neatly frames the honey-coloured hexagonal belltower of the church of **Santa Catalina** (Mon–Sat 10.30am–1.45pm, 5.30–7.15pm, Sun 11am–2pm, 6–7pm; free) in a square of the same name. Built over a mosque, it was thought to be baroque until restoration work revealed the original Gothic shell. A sculpture embedded horizontally in the wall at the back, on Plaça Lope de Vega, suggests building methods were haphazard. The coquettishly graceful baroque belltower remains one of the city's best-loved landmarks. Look closely at the unique little cupola on the top and you will see that it is sculpted with stone fish scales.

Just outside Santa Catalina, on Sombrerería, are two old-fashioned cafés, El Siglo and Santa Catalina. Take your pick between home-made *orxata/ horchata* (tiger-nut milk), or drinking chocolate with *fartons*, spongy sweet fingers of bread for dipping.

Seminary Treasures

It is a 10-minute walk from Santa Catalina to **El Patriarca**, as local people call the 16th-century Royal Seminary College of Corpus Christi (Carrer Nau/Calle Nave 1). Here, young trainee priests still go about their business. The real treasures are in the library (not open to the public) and the **museum** (daily 11am–1.30pm; small admission fee). Both owe their existence to Andalusian theologian Juan Ribera, the Patriarca who founded the seminary. He was the king's viceroy, the city's archbishop and a highly respected man of learning. The manuscripts he bought for the library included

Above: Santa Catalina's belltower
Right: El Patriarca's Corpus Christi church

Sir Thomas More's final work, written in prison before he was executed. Facsimiles are on sale in the lobby.

Ribera also commissioned paintings from leading artists of the day. They are on show in the small but fabulous art museum, reached via a grand, beautifully tiled two-storey Renaissance patio. Packed into one small room are 50 outstanding paintings by artists from Valencian Joan de Joanes to El Greco. There is also a late 16th-century map of the world.

El Patriarca's church of **Corpus Christi** (daily 8–11am, 1–2pm, 7–8pm) is almost entirely covered with colourful frescoes by Bernabé Matarana. Just outside the main door hangs a dried, stuffed alligator given to Ribera by the Viceroy of Peru in 1606. (Since alligators do not have tongues they symbolised the virtues of silence.) The church is known for its Gregorian chant, sung every day except Monday at 10am. A full-day sung liturgy, held on the Thursday after Corpus Christi (in June), packs the church.

Gilt and Graffito

Among the old town's other churches, **Sant Esteve** (Mon–Sat 8.30–9am, 6.45–8.30pm; Sun most of the day), in Plaça Sant Esteve, has highly original baroque decoration. Sant Vicent Ferrer, the city's patron saint, was baptised here, making it popular for baptisms today. Today, the walls and ceiling are almost entirely covered by duck-egg blue and white decorative *esgraffito*, a style for which local architect Juan Perez Castiel was famous. The effect, finished off with gold rosettes, stone cherubs and sculpted garlanded arches, is like a richly iced cake.

Midweek, you can extend the walk to the **Cripta Arqueológic de Sant Vicent Màrtir** (Tues–Sat 9.30am–2pm, 5.30–8pm; Sun 9.30am–2pm; admission fee) in Plaça del Arquebisbe, located just behind the cathedral. Here are various excavated ruins, the most notable of which is a 7th-century Visigoth funerary chapel with a beautiful, almost intact, carved stone altar. During Muslim times the chapel was employed as a bath-house. There is an option to join a 25-minute child-friendly multimedia show telling the story of ancient Valencia, but it is more atmospheric to see the chapel quietly on your own.

10. THE OLD TOWN'S PLAÇAS BY NIGHT
(see map, p24)

A stroll after dark allows you to appreciate the old town's fountains, sculptures and monuments, many of which are spectacularly illuminated. Along the way you will find cafés where you can pause for a drink and try the city's very own orange-juice cocktail.

The **Plaça de la Mare de Déu**, transformed at night by its brightly lit fountain, seems to glow in the dark. The sensuality of the reclining male nude and eight nubile Valencian maidens, who symbolise the River Turia and the city's eight irrigation channels, are slightly kitsch by day but seem to fit perfectly at night. You can sit and watch life go by from one of the cafés in the square, or you can walk round to the back of the cathedral and enjoy the quietly trickling fountain in the peaceful **Plaça de l'Arquebisbe**.

From the Plaça de la Mare de Déu, Carrer Cavallers leads towards the hectic nightlife zone of El Carme. You could spend an entire evening exploring nightspots in this lamp-lit street. After crossing Plaça de Manises – which is quiet and shadowy at night – the first turning on the left, Carrer Calatrava, takes you to the **Plaça del Negret** (Plaza del Negrito), a tiny square where a fat cherub sits atop a fountain spouting water into a scallop shell. The plaza's café is a favourite spot for a drink outside on summer evenings.

Illuminated Buildings

Keep on down Calatrava, passing a lovely restored Renaissance house in the next square, and you will come out on Plaça Doctor Collado, where the Café Lisboa's tables are laid out under an olive tree. Turn right down the back of the 16th-century Silk Exchange, La Llotja, to see the details of its carving and the crown-shaped crenellations on its patio wall. The next short alleyway to the left leads to the **Plaça del Mercat**. In medieval times this was the site of one of the city's main gates, and it was here that bullfights and inquisition burnings took place. The illumination on **Sants Joans** church, facing La Llotja, makes its Italian frieze look spectacular.

From here it is just five minutes' walk via Carrer Trench, a small street that turns left off the Plaça del Mercat, to the little round **Plaça Redonda**. At night

Above: Plaça de la Mare de Déu

the fountain's four spouts splash quietly under a lamp in the centre. If you walk through **Carrer de la Pescatería** on the opposite side you will emerge on Carrer Sant Vicent Martír. Facing you is the church of Sant Martí (San Martín) – badly in need of a good clean. Down the right-hand side Abadia de Sant Martí leads to the **Palau de Dos Aigües** with its rich rococo façade. It is worth a special visit to see its details picked out by night-time illumination. Do not miss the elegant fountain, like a three-tiered cake-stand, around the corner.

A few buildings back up from the Palau, on Abadia de Sant Martí, stands the Café de Madrid, which is said to be the birthplace of Aigüa de Valencia, the city's famous cocktail, dreamed up during an artists' and writers' drinking session here in the bohemian days of the 1970s. Served in small glass jugs and made up to order from a secret recipe involving fresh orange juice, *Cava* (the Spanish version of champagne) and four sweet liqueurs, it slips down easily but packs a punch.

Ducks in Water

To see one last fountain, head down to Carrer Pau (Calle Paz) and cut through to the Plaça de Sant Vicent Ferrer. Locally known as **Plaça de los Patos** after the diminutive ducks who spout water into the central fountain, it makes a romantic set-piece, backed by the richly coloured façade of Sant Tomás i Sant Felip Neri, the 19th-century church to the north the square.

For dinner try Abadia D'Espi (En Sala 3, tel: 96 351 20 77; *see page 68*), an excellent small restaurant near the Palau de Dos Aigües, which serves updated versions of traditional cuisine. It is often full so it is a good idea to book. A stone's throw from the Plaça de Sant Vicent Ferrer is La Ríua (Del Mar 27, tel: 96 391 45 71), which offers good local food at reasonable prices.

Above: preparing Aigüa de Valencia in the Café de Madrid
Right: a bottle to take home

excursions

Excursions

11. A STROLL IN THE HUERTA   *(see map, p54)*

Almàssera's Museu de l'Horta reveals the rural ways of life that shaped the picturesque landscape of the city's market gardens. Afterwards you can take a stroll or cycle through the mosaic of fields and enjoy a glass of *orxata*, tiger-nut milk, a speciality of these farming towns.

The **Museu de L'Horta** (Tues–Fri 10am–1pm, 5–8pm, Sat 11am–1pm, 5–8pm; free), on Avinguda del Mar, is just 10 minutes' walk from Almàssera metro (L3), signposted down the road running towards the sea. If you are feeling energetic, you can take a bicycle on the metro free of charge *(for bike-hire details, see page 82)*. The flat alluvial plain here is perfect cycling country.

Here you will find yourself surrounded by *l'horta*, or *la huerta*, the city's famous irrigated market gardens planted in the coastal plain's fertile soil. Urban development has eaten its way through large areas of the chequerboard of small fields and gardens, but in this area the picturesque flat landscape remains well conserved.

Muslim Farmstead

The 19th-century whitewashed-stone museum, which was once the town's slaughterhouse, has been restored along the lines of an *alquería*, one of the self-sufficient farmsteads built by the Muslims who first laid out and cultivated the fields here. The design endured and became typical of the area's later, wealthier farmsteads. Inside, on the right-hand side, you will find a typical well, a hearth and a tiled kitchen, together with ceramic jars used for storing rice, olive oil and wine. Sausage-making equipment, ingenious home-made toys and old-fashioned cleaning equipment are also on display.

The other side of the museum is dedicated to farming and, in particular, to the tiger nuts, or *xufas*, that grow in more than half of Almàssera's fields. They are dried and ground to make sweet tiger-nut milk, called *orxata (horchata)*. Photographic displays show how they used to be sown, harvested, cleaned and then sorted by hand. Today the crop survives, and tiger-nut milk remains a Valencian hot-weather speciality, although farming methods have been mechanised.

Outside, at the back of the museum, small beds of Mediterranean herbs and vegetables are grown traditionally – in other words, organically – and next to

Left: patchwork agricultural landscape around Valencia. **Right:** Almàssera farmer

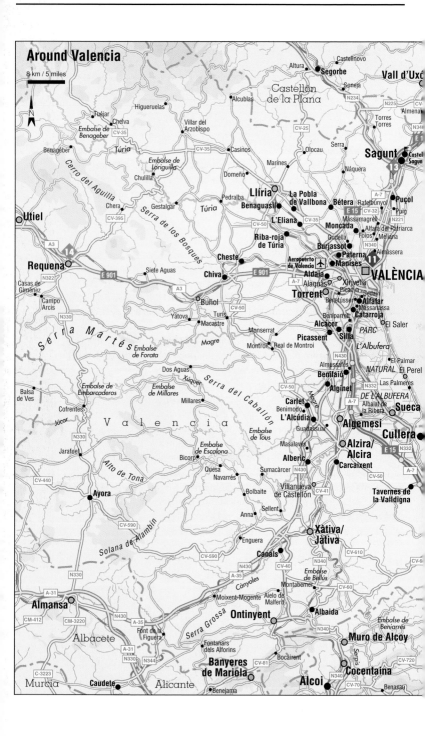

them are small covered chicken, pigeon and rabbit houses. Here you can see the typical local breeds, such as the huge Valencian rabbit.

From the museum, a clearly marked red cycle path allows you to walk or cycle through the fields. It leads you east of the museum, initially running down the road, as if continuing to the marina of Port Sa Playa, but soon turning off it north (left) along the signed Camí Via Xurra. Here you can still see working farmsteads. Traditionally, palms were planted to give shade over front doors and fences were made out of cane. Around the fine, rich clay fields run water courses with small gates, which are opened during the time-slot when each farmer is allowed to irrigate. Apart from vegetables, tiger nuts and other cash crops, each farmstead also had its own orange, lemon, fig, carob and olive trees. As Rose Macaulay wrote in the 1930s: 'It all looks smiling and fruity and very well-watered.'

A Walk to the Tiger Nuts

The network of paths here between Almàssera and Meliana allows you to walk or cycle for as long as you like. Alternatively, or afterwards, you can take the Camí Via Xurra south towards neighbouring Alboraia, famous for the quality of its tiger-nut milk. The walk here takes you across a small canal-like river before entering the outskirts of Alboraia. You can turn east here down the riverside path to the sea. After 10 minutes you will come to the main road, where a sign marks the site of the Vía Augusta, the Roman coastal highway. Turning right, it is a 25-minute walk or 10-minute cycle ride through the centre of Alboraia to the cafés selling tiger-nut milk. Follow the signs in town to the Avinguda de la Orxata (Avenida de la Horchata).

If you don't have the energy or time to walk, you can travel back by metro to Palmaret, where you will emerge directly on Avinguda de la Orxata. Facing you is Spain's most famous *orxatería*, **Daniel** (Apr–Sept daily 10am–midnight; Oct–Dec 4–10pm). You will usually find a long queue at the take-away counter. In the large café you can try the tiger-nut milk chilled, or as a *granizada* (a granita-like icy slush), or mixed with another iced drink, such as coffee, lemon or barley water. Alternatively, there are wonderful home-made ice creams and local sundaes, including *blanc i negra* (white and black), a mixture of vanilla ice cream and coffee granita.

If you would prefer a full-scale meal, take a taxi from Almàssera to El Famós, a large farmstead converted into a tavern-like restaurant (Camí de Vera s/n, tel: 96 371 00 28; open Tues–Sun lunch), which stands next to the **Ermita de Vera**, an old chapel open on Sunday morning. El Famós (The Famous One) serves delicious good-value grilled meat and traditional paella with rabbit, snails and chicken, all cooked over a wood fire. After your meal they will book you a taxi for the 10-minute ride back into town.

Right: serving *orxata*

12. L'ALBUFERA *(see map below)*

To the south of the city lies L'Albufera, a vast freshwater lake protected within a natural park. Here you can visit a wildlife centre and bird observatory, lunch in a fishing village surrounded by rice paddies, walk on sandy dunes with wild pine groves and take a boat ride on the lake at sunset. The changing seasons make it interesting throughout the year.

'The birds do not fit in the sky, nor the fish in the water,' wrote Gaspar Aguilar to Felipe II after visiting L'Albufera in 1599. At that time the lake, over six times its present size, was reserved as a royal hunting ground, although El Palmar, a small village on an island in the lake, held the rights to fish for its plentiful eels and grey mullet. Four hundred years later L'Albufera is surrounded by swathes of rice fields planted on land reclaimed since the 18th century. Pollution from nearby factories has taken a heavy toll, but today, 20 years after a natural park was set up, 80 bird species nest in the lake's reedy fringes and islands, and 30 different species of fish swim here.

The natural park covers a total of 21,000ha (51,890 acres) and is

Above: a boat trip on L'Albufera

designed to protect not only the lake but also its related ecosystems – the marshy surrounds, the rice paddies and the sandy dunes dividing it from the sea. Villages and towns such as El Saler, El Palmar and El Perelló, on the eastern side, and Catarroja on the western side, also lie within it. The landscapes here go through startling seasonal transformations and are perhaps at their most beautiful when the rice fields are flooded, between November and January, or when they turn a rich emerald green between June and July. For birdwatchers, the spring nesting season is the ideal time to make a visit.

Getting Around the Park

The best way to see all the different ecosystems in one day is to hire a car. (There is a local bus along the eastern side of the lake, from Valencia to El Perelló, stopping at El Saler and turning off into El Palmar. It leaves from Plaça Cánovas del Castillo and runs seven times a day on weekdays; check times with the tourist offices as they vary. The trip takes 30 minutes out to El Palmar, and 90 minutes back, as you loop south to El Perelló. Another solution is the Albufera Bus Turistic, which leaves from Plaça de la Reina three times a day in summer and four times in winter – again, check times with the tourist office. The two-hour tour to El Palmar includes a 30-minute boat ride and a glimpse of the dunes.) It is not a good idea to walk or cycle from Valencia, or between El Palmar and El Saler, because the highway is crowded and narrow, without a cycle path or pavement.

Hiring a car allows a much fuller itinerary. Taking the city-centre road that runs along the river's south bank past the City of Arts and Sciences (Alcalde Reig) you soon enter the park. After reaching the rice paddies, the road runs between the lake and pine dunes. If you take the turn-off to El Palmar, after about 14km (8 miles), you come almost immediately to the **Centro de Información e Interpretación del Parc Natural L'Albufera** (daily 9am–2pm, also Tues and Thur 4–6.30pm in summer, 4–5.30pm in winter; tel: 96 162 30 33). For a complete visit, which includes three walking itineraries, allow approximately two hours. One itinerary includes an audio-visual museum, with mul-

tilingual soundtracks, explaining the origins of the lake in a huge bay; another one leads to a birdwatching hide. Some 250 bird species visit the lake during the course of a year, and you are almost sure to see herons, but you may also spot various members of the duck and seagull family in winter, terns in summer, various waders and even, perhaps, the marble teal, an endangered species.

From here it is just a 3-km (2-mile) drive to El Palmar. You can leave your car in a large, dusty car park before walking round the tiny grid of village streets. In 1855 a fire burned down most of the old clay-walled, rush-roofed *barracas*. The few that survive are best seen from the lake on a boat trip in one of the traditional *barquets*, or flat-bottomed fishing boats, which are designed to negotiate the shallow waters. Close to the car park, for example, is the Embarcadero El Tío Pastilla, which is open every day of the year. A 30-minute ride costs €4, but you can also phone in advance and reserve longer, tailor-made trips (tel: 96 162 02 86). Around sunset is the best time of day to organise a trip – the play of light on the glassy water is beautiful even if you do not catch one of the famous technicolour sunsets.

Restaurant Specialities

Many Valencians now drive out to El Palmar just to eat the local fish and rice dishes in the two dozen restaurants that have sprung up here. Specialities include peppery-hot stewed eel *(all-i-pebre)*, paella with rabbit or duck, and grey mullet *(llisa)*, but each restaurant has its own variants. If these don't appeal, you can also get delicious *parrilladas*, or grilled Mediter-

ranean vegetables. If you are going out for lunch at the weekend it is definitely advisable to book ahead – one good choice is Mateu (Vicente Baldoví 17, tel: 96 162 02 70), a family restaurant that serves everything from traditional rice dishes to luxury shellfish stews.

If you have booked a boat for sunset, you can spend the afternoon wandering around the village. It has kept its rice wholesalers, wharf, lateen-sailed boats and Comunidad de Pescadores, which has organised the annual lottery for fishing rights since the 13th century. Women were allowed to enter the lottery for the first time in 2001. You will often see fishing nets drying around the wharves, and the canes staking out each fisherman's plot are clearly visible in the water.

Alternatively, you could drive back along the isthmus that links El Palmar to the lake's shore, take the road back to Valencia, and turn into the Dehesa, the 10-km (6-mile) strip of dunes between the sea and the lake. It offers wonderful walking among wild pines and maritime vegetation. You can also drive on towards the southern end of the lake. After a few kilometres you will see the world-famous El Saler golf course and, at El Perelló, you can see one of the three locks that regulate the lake's level, allowing the water to rise and flood the rice fields in winter.

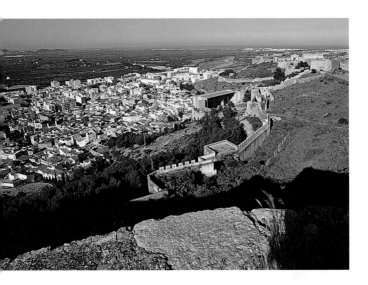

13. SAGUNT *(see map, p54)*

The town of Sagunt (Sagunto in Castilian) sits below an imposing, flat-topped hill, where a castle precinct encircles the site of Iberian, Roman and Muslim cities. There is also a Roman theatre and medieval quarter dotted with Classical fragments. A bus ride away, at Sagunt port, you can walk on the beach, swim and eat lunch.

Sagunt lies 23km (14 miles) north of Valencia on the train route to Castelló de la Plana. Trains leave the Estació del Nord at least every 30 minutes throughout the day and evening, and the journey, through small coastal towns and citrus orchards, takes 29 minutes.

From the station, where there is a good coffee bar, it is a 15-minute walk to the centre of town along the Camí Reial. When you come to Plaça Cronista Chabret on your right, a turning to the left takes you into the *ciutat vella*, the old town. First, pick up the useful maps of Sagunt town and port from the tourist office in a kiosk at the far end of the square. Almost as soon as you enter the old town you come to the **Plaça Major** (Plaza Mayor), where Roman columns have been recycled in the arcade of the town's market.

Roman Theatre

Leaving the church of Santa María off to your right, Carrer Castell runs up towards the semicircular **Teatre Romà** (Tues–Sat 10am–8pm, Sun 10am–2pm; free), built between the 1st and 3rd centuries AD. Registered as a national monument in 1896, it was, unfortunately, encased in cement and brick in the 1990s. A Supreme Court decision paralysed the work, but it came too late. The result is today's curious Modernist hybrid. During August a series of evening concerts and shows are held here. At the back of the auditorium, the old tunnelled accesses remain more or less intact and are fun to explore.

Above left: a heron in L'Albufera. **Left:** on the sands at El Saler
Above: Sagunt from the castle precinct

From the theatre it is another steep 10-minute walk up the approach road to the **Castell de Sagunt** (summer: daily 10am–8pm; winter: until 6.30pm). The hilltop site, which is surrounded by walls nearly 1km (⅓ mile) long, retains a wild, unkempt magic. Guides are sometimes on hand in July and August to decode the ruins. The rest of the year you are left to wander as you like.

The 360-degree views over the sea, coastal plain and mountains are absolutely splendid. On the highest point stood the Iberian port of Arse, which flowered under Roman protection until Hannibal laid siege to it in 219BC and then, nine months later, razed it to the ground. Its destruction triggered the Second Punic War, which led to the fall of the Carthaginians in Europe. Three centuries later the Romans rebuilt the town, which they called Saguntum, and it became their most important outpost on this stretch of the Mediterranean. Civic monuments were built on the hilltop; below, closer to the river, lay houses and the circus. The Muslims used the same hilltop site to build a defensive fortress within a larger walled town called Murbitar, from the Visigothic name Mur Viedro, meaning old wall. This became corrupted to Morvedre, which remained the name of the medieval town, and only in 1868 did it change back to Sagunt.

Museum Collection

It takes an hour to visit the entire precinct. As you enter, you find the Roman forum, taverns, courthouse and Republican temple. At the precinct's highest point are the few remaining ruins of the Iberian town, around the so-called Tower of Hercules. The archaeological finds here are being prepared for a new museum inside the Casa del Mestre Penya in the old town below. It will also show Muslim ceramics and Jewish jewellery.

On the slope below the castle is the excavated Jewish cemetery, which sits directly above the **Judería**, or Jewish quarter, one of the largest and best preserved in Spain. Entry is marked by the **Portalet de la Sang**, an arched gateway on Calle Castillo.

Back down by the Plaça Major the town's most central church, Santa María, was built between the 14th and 18th centuries. If you are nearby when it opens for mass (8.30am and 7pm, before mass begins), it is worth

Above right: Sagunt's old town
Above left: ceramics shop in the old town

a look inside. Equally intriguing is the so-called **Temple de Diana** (Calle Sagrario), a 4th- to 5th-century BC wall thought to have formed a podium or base for an Iberian-Roman temple. Other interesting Roman fragments – a chunk of the Vía Augustus and the door into the circus – are scattered around the lower town and marked on the tourist map.

On the Beach

For lunch, a good gourmet option close to the castle is L'Armeler (Carrer Castell 44, tel: 96 266 43 82), a small restaurant specialising in game. For fish and seafood, make the 4-km (2½-mile) trip to Sagunt beach and port for lunch and a swim. A direct bus (No 102d) makes a circular route, leaving from a clearly marked bus stop on the riverside Avinguda Sants de la Pedra (daily 8am–9.30pm; Sat on the hour and half hour; Sun on the half-hour only). From the bus you will see the huge iron furnace, a monument to the town's foundry, around which a museum will grow. There is a good choice of restaurants along Avenida del Mediterráneo.

If you decide to spend a night here to enjoy the small beach, the cheerful, modern, three-star Hotel Vent de Mar (Isla de Córcega 61, tel: 96 269 80 84, fax: 96 267 05 35; €€) a few streets from the sea, is a good choice.

14. REQUENA: A WINE TOWN   *(see map, p54)*

Requena is easily reached by train from Valencia. Its medieval quarter has survived as a tightly packed network of quiet streets, underneath which runs a warren of underground caves. After visiting them you can enjoy a country-style lunch washed down by excellent local wines.

Three trains leave from the Estació del Nord in the morning, and two return in the afternoon; times vary according to the day of the week; the journey time is about 1½ hours. In summer it is best to take the earliest train to avoid walking around in the midday heat.

The train from Valencia to Requena cuts through lovely countryside. Lush citrus groves climb to wild rolling hills and red farmland rimmed by high sierras. You enter a carpet of vines before El Rebollar. Some 15 minutes further is Requena; leave the train here and make the 10-minute walk to the town centre, where a square watchtower at the end of Avenida Arrabal marks the entrance to **El Barrio de La Villa**, the medieval town, erected on a promontory. This fortress, built in Arab times and called Rakkana, which means strong and

Right: La Villa, Requena's old town

safe, gave the town its name. Strategically positioned overlooking the high plains linking Valencia to Castile, it fostered the growth of the small Arabic hilltop town. After the reconquest, the Christian town slowly outgrew the medina walls, churches were added and older buildings were embellished. Wealth from silk production during the 18th century– there were 800 looms here – was followed by a long economic decline. Today it is prosperous once more, thanks to the revival of the vineyards, and it retains a special character, part Valencian and part Castilian.

Exploring La Villa

You need about an hour to explore La Villa's unbroken web of narrow alleys. Maps are available from the tourist office just below the fortress, on García Montés, or you can simply be guided by street signs. Santa María, the main Muslim and medieval street, runs right down La Villa's eastern side, passing the Plaza del Pozo, where the silk-weavers' guild was based. Further down, on the left, is the splendid 14th-century doorway of **Santa María** church, due to open for visits when restoration work finishes. Further down is **Somera de Arriba**, where a 15th-century Gothic palace named after El Cid is being converted into a wine museum. Right at the end of the old town, close to San Nicolás church, tiny atmospheric alleys run beneath archways to the edge of the hill looking down on the modern town below.

The visit to the **Cuevas de la Villa** (town caves; Tues–Sun tours at 11am, noon, 1pm; Fri–Sun also 4.15pm, 5pm and 6pm; admission fee) is another surprise. The entrance is on the central main square, Plaza de Albornoz. Underneath runs a warren of caves tunnelled out of the porous tufa rock between the 8th and 10th centuries. Ever since they have found various uses, from wine cellars to wartime refuge. The tour lasts about 40 minutes.

Taste the Wine

Wine is now the backbone of the town's economy. Most vineyards were planted after phylloxera destroyed the coastal vineyards at the beginning

Above: Mesón del Vino
Right: vineyards outside Requena

of the 20th century, but more recently they have come into their own, thanks to a wave of investment in new technology and the rediscovery of the region's big fruity Bobal grape. Now the fame and value of local wines, sold under the Utiel-Requena DO *(Denominació d'Origen)*, are rising fast. A good place to try them is at Pedro Moreno (García Montés 21; Tues–Sat 10.30am–2pm, 5–8.30pm, Sun 11am–1.30pm), just below the old town.

Around the Market

On Saturday morning you can dawdle until 2pm in the busy food and street market in the new town and visit the **Museo Municipal** (Tues–Sun 11am–2pm; admission fee), at Músico Sosa 1. It contains a potpourri of items, from Roman archaeological finds to 19th-century farmhouse furniture and local costumes. Almost next door to the market is a large old inn, Mesón del Vino (Avenida Arrabal 11, tel: 96 230 00 01), where regulars eat leisurely country lunches washed down with the local red wine. Cooking is a mixture of Valencian and Castilian country cuisine. Dishes include the spicy pork pâté called *morteruelo*, a cold potato, garlic and salt-cod purée called *ajo arriero* and lots of pork sausages, or *embutidos*. House wine is delicious, but you may like to ask the waiter to pick out one of the area's best Reservas.

A privately owned 16th-century water-powered flour mill, restored to working order, is a final sight. Called the **Molino de Ester** (tel: 96 230 57 13), it can be found on the edge of town close to the railway station, at the end of Calle Dr Fleming, over a small bridge and down a track leading to the river. The municipal museum will ring ahead to arrange a time for a visit.

Requena also makes a good base for a two-day trip visiting and tasting wine at the vineyards. A characterful place to stay is the Cantón del Ángel (Somera de Arriba 48, tel: 650 428 717), a lovely converted house in the old town's alleyways. The Requena wine authority is currently drawing up a Ruta de Vino, detailing visits to small wine museums and *bodegas*.

One of Europe's longest footpaths, the GR-7, runs through this area. A short walk along it takes you back to the railway line at El Rebollar in the middle of the vineyards, where you can pick up the train back to Valencia.

excursions

Leisure Activities

SHOPPING

…alencia's shops are conveniently clustered. …lost crafts are found in or close to the old …rt of town. Designer home goods, expen…ve fashion and jewellery are concentrated …n Pau (Paz) and Poeta Querol, while high-…reet fashion shops line Colom (Colón) and, …nning off it, Russafa. Close by is the Mer-…at de Colom, which has lots of upmarket gift …nd fashion shops in and around it. Head …r the Barri del Carme (Barrio del Carmen) …r alternative, young home-grown fashion. …pening times are generally 10am–1.30 or …pm and 4.30 or 5–8pm, except for food …hops and markets, which are usually open …y 9am. The annual Christmas shopping …ree comes to a climax on 5 January, when …hops are busy till well after midnight.

Ceramics and Other Crafts

…here is a good selection of local ceramics …nd fabrics in the **Plaça Redonda** *(see Mar-…ets)*. **Yuste**, at Plaça Miracle Mocaoret 5, …st off Plaça de la Reina, is a more serious …fair, selling crafts and antique and new …eramic tiles, including *socorrats*, thick, …aked-clay slabs. **Lladró**, at Poeta Querol 9, … collected around the world, but the design … strictly for certain tastes (you can also visit …eir workshops in Tavernes Blanques). For …andles, go to **Cirios Felipe** (Navellos 14), …lose to the cathedral, a wonderful old shop. …ativity figures and pots are sold at **Peréz …lartínez** (Drets/Derechos 4 and Chofrens …), where there is an amazing range of reli-…ious objects, nativity figures and metal pots. …here is a great selection of rope-soled shoes …nd wooden items at Alero Mimbres, Musico …eydró 18.

…ashion

…he big names of Spanish high-street fash-…on are within a stone's throw of one another: …ara (Colom 11 and 18), **Mango** (Colom …) and **Camper**, the stylish foot-friendly

Mallorcan shoemakers (Colom 13). Prices are around a third cheaper than outside Spain. **Women's Secret** (Colom 66–67), is a newer lingerie and nightwear chain. Span-ish designer fashion includes **Carolina Her-rera** (Pau/Paz 13), **Loewe** (Poeta Querol 7 and Marqués de Dos Aigües 7), Catalan designer **Armand Basi** (Colom 52) and Valencian **Francisco Montesinos** (Comte de Salvatierra 25). They are all expensive. Less pricy are **Loreak** (Joaquín Costa 11), a hip, good-value Basque design label; **La Room**, slightly off the beaten track (Cordellats 6),

with funky original T-shirts; and VDG **Jóvenes Diseñadores** (Calatrava 9), which stocks affordable and fun local designs. Imported surf wear can be found on Cav-allers, Cuarte and Bossería. There is good skateboard fashion at **Skate World** (Comédies 14). On Sant Vicent Martír a trio of old-fashioned shops sells stylish tradi-tional accessories – fans, embroidered silk shawls, umbrellas and walking sticks. **Ros-alén**, at No 19 and Nela, at No 2, both have

eft: La Tomatina, an extraordinary tomato-throwing festival held in late August
light: Valencian fashion

a great selection. The best fans and shawls are not cheap – they can run to more than €300. Close to the station is a great old hat shop, **Albero** (Xàtiva 21). If you want to go the whole way and buy a *Fallas* outfit *(see page 74)* – women's embroidered silk dresses and shoes, and men's short white trousers and red cummerbunds – try **Siglo XVIII** (Avellanas 3) and Indumentaria Dos Aguas (Mar 20).

Jewellery
For chic, baroque-style local silver, gold and jewels try **Gracia** (Pau/Paz 4 and Russafa 29). They also stock Lalique and other brands. Almost next door, at Pau 16, is **Pajarón**, a centennial business with its own hand-made jewellery. Younger silver jewellery design is at **8m²** (Bossería 28).

Food, Wine and Cigars
At the **Mercat Central** (Plaça del Mercat 6) you can buy saffron, *jamón* (cured ham), either whole or sliced and vacuum-packed, farmhouse cheeses and cold cuts. The stalls at the front of the market sell paella pans and Mediterranean kitchen equipment. There are two great shops making their own hand-crafted *turrón*, the almond-based Christmas sweet: Turrones Galiana (Plaça del Ajuntament 3), and Turrones Ramos (Sombrerería 11). Choose between halva-like and hard white nougat types, plus crystallised fruit (a speciality here), marzipans and honeys. Close to the railway station, **Las Añadas de España** (Xátiva 3) is a fabulous wine shop with gourmet goodies. **Joaquín Muñoz** (Moratín 11) is a family run treasure trove with a huge range o cigars. Local chocolate lovers swear by the truffles at **Trufas Martínez** (Russafa 12).

Picnic Shopping
Apart from the range at the central marke *(see above)*, there are wonderful bakeries around town, selling savoury pies, breads cakes and biscuits. Centrally, try **Las Comedias** (Comédies 11), just off Pau.

Home Design and Antiques
Bañón (Lauria 28, Plaça del Ajuntament 1 and Sant Vicent 59) is the main loca designer haven – it has good stock at fai prices. **La Oca** (Poeta Quintana 3–5) stock more expensive but very good Catala design. For antiques, head for Avellane and Purísima.

Music and Books
A good one-stop depot for music, DVDs books (some English-language stock) an newspapers is **FNAC** (Guillem de Castro 9 Pick up a local instrument at **Union Musi cal Española** (Pau 29).

Original Presents and Souvenirs
A visit to the **Valencia football club sho** (Pintor Sorolla 25) is a good solution t present-buying problems for any keen foo ball fan. For others, instead of buying brande perfume at the duty-free shop, try the fabu lous old-fashioned natural eau-de-cologn

Above: pottery for sale in Plaça de la Reina. **Above right**: paella pans on sale near the market
Right: Nela, a specialist fan-makers

d other products at **Cosméticos Paquita**
rs (Pau 27 and Sant Vicent 65). **Mur Mur**
laça del Mercat 32) has amusing designer
uvenir candles, fans and watches.

Museum shops are found in **IVAM**, at the
rdí Botanic *(see page 27)* and, in the town
entre, in the old **Universitat** building (La
au, Universitat 2). They have their own
esign home and stationery ranges as well as
xcellent visual books. Their hours coin-
de with the museum opening hours.

rt Galleries

alencia is famed for its buzzy art scene.
eading galleries include **La Nava** (Nau 25),
r 20th-century Spanish artists such as
casso and Miró; **Luis Adelantado** (Bonaire
), for young international names; **Tomás**
larch (Aparisi y Guijarro 7), for current
panish artists; and **My Name is Lolita**
Avellanes 7) for Spanish revival pop.

Markets

he **Plaça Redonda**, known locally as El
lot, in the alleyways just off Plaça Lopez
e Vega, is a gem, with stalls open Monday
 Saturday; on Sunday it becomes a caged
ird and pet market. There is a true flea
arket, held next to the main football
tadium, **Camp de Mestalla**, in the **Plaça**
uis Casanova, off Avinguda de Suecia,
arting early on Sunday morning; lots of
nk, bargains and eccentric collectables are
vailable. Every Thursday morning, the

Mercadillo de Cabanyal is a fun, sprawling market for cheap clothes and shoes, with
plants and other items, too. On Tuesday
morning a clothes market, **Mercat de**
Jerusalem, sprawls on and around Convento
de Jerusalem, next to the railway station.
On summer Sundays and evenings street
market stalls are laid out along the beach at
Malva Rosa.

Department Stores

El Corte Inglés (Colom 1; Mon–Sat 10am–
10pm), Europe's most profitable department
store, brings everything traditional under
one roof, from clothing to household goods,
at a price, and it arranges VAT-free export
outside Europe.

EATING OUT

Valencia's cuisine goes well beyond paella, its most famous dish. This is the heartland of real Mediterranean cooking, and there are fabulous vegetable dishes, excellent (but expensive) seafood, tapas and cheeses, and big, fruity wines from up-and-coming local producing areas such as Utiel Requena.

Nonetheless, rice dishes are a good starting point. Paella is one of dozens – among others are *arros negre* (rice with squid ink, which makes it black) and *fideuà*, a pasta version of seafood paella. Drop by the local markets if you would like to see the full array of fish, citrus fruits and local vegetables grown in the famed *hortas*, or market gardens.

The city's restaurant culture is also young and open in spirit. Italian, French, Moroccan and Oriental cooking are all well represented, and younger Valencian chefs' modern cuisine is starting to shine. A newer city-centre breed of venues also offers food alongside art, music and the occasional DJ. Traditional tapas – small, appetising dishes – are an unbeatable, if sometimes expensive, option *(see page 71)*.

In summer the delicious ice creams and cold drinks such as *orxata (horchata)*, or tiger-nut milk, and *granizada*, an icy slush, made from lemon and barley water, come into their own. They are at their best when freshly hand-made *(artesanal)*.

Eating times usually run from 1 or 1.30–4pm and 9–11.30pm, although most local people do not eat lunch till 2pm or dinner till 10pm. A number of restaurants, especially family businesses, close on Sunday evening, Monday and for two weeks or the who[le] month of August. Phone to check in advanc[e.]

Prices are generally very reasonable, eve[n] at the Michelin-starred level. Restaura[nt] prices are graded: **€** = inexpensive, €6–2[0;] **€€** = moderate, €20–50; **€€€** = expensiv[e,] above €50.

Cathedral and Market Quarter[s]

Fast-food and touristy restaurants may see[m] to rule the day on the big plazas, but there a[re] good local eating venues in the side street[s,] especially close to the market.

Abadia D'Espi
En Sala 3
Tel: 96 351 20 77
Just off Calle Pau, this is an elegant restaura[nt] that serves regional cooking with a moder[n] twist and has a really excellent wine lis[t.] *Fideuà* is a speciality. Closed at weekends. **€**[€]

Bar de la Llotja
Palafox 1
Tel: 96 351 13 34
A family-owned restaurant next to the Centra[l] Market. It serves genuine paella, excelle[nt] three-course lunches and other unpretentiou[s] food to a local crowd. Lunch only. **€**

La Lola
Pujada del Toledà (Subida del Toledano)
Tel: 96 391 80 45
Sixties pop décor sets the tone for this restaurant right by the cathedral. The cooking i[s] modern Mediterranean. It's a good spot fo[r] a night out – there are drinks and DJs fro[m] midnight. **€€€**

La Riuà
Del Mar 27
Tel: 96 391 45 71/96 391 71 72
A good spot near the Glorieta to sample local
cooking, especially a range of local rice plates.
A typical three-course set menu might be a
rice dish, fish and pumpkin custard. **€€**

Ocho y Medio
Plaça Lope de Vega 5
Tel: 96 392 20 22
Creative upmarket cooking with foie gras
a speciality and wines from all over the
world. Live jazz at weekends. Booking
essential. **€€**

El Barri del Carme

This area, the hub of Valencia's nightlife,
is packed with good places to eat, ranging
from wonderful tapas bars to sharp, avant-
garde Spanish restaurants.

Café Bar Pilar
Moro Zeit 13
Tel: 96 391 04 97
Nearly a century old, this bar is usually
packed with local people enjoying the mus-
sels *(clóchinas)* and other delicious tapas.
Open all year from noon till midnight. **€**

Ca'n Bermell
Sant Tomás 18
Tel: 96 391 02 88
A city-centre classic with fabulous Valencian
cooking, an unfussy atmosphere and good service. Dishes range from braised peppers to
poached eggs with truffles and foie gras. **€€**

Dukala
Nogueros 5
Tel: 96 392 62 53
Excellent Moroccan bistro dishes, such as
freshly made couscous, and date rolls with
orange salad – plus a good, short Spanish
wine list. Dinner only mid-week. Booking
advisable. **€€**

La Carme
Mosén Sorell 7
Tel: 96 392 25 32
One of the quarter's oldest restaurants serves
innovative Spanish cuisine at accessible
prices. Dinner only. **€€**

La Dispensa della Nonna
Plaça Santa Ursula 3
Tel: 96 392 26 29
This small, quiet, cosmopolitan Italian café
next to the Torres de Cuart serves good pasta,
salads and carpaccio. Open all year. **€€**

La Sucursal,
IVAM
Guillem de Castro 11
Tel: 96 374 66 65
A smart new museum restaurant serving top-
flight cooking to a mixed business and arts
crowd. Try dishes such as rabbit in cocoa-
bean and apple sauce. The café downstairs
serves budget price, but good, Mediterranean
café food. **€€€**

Osteria de Vicolo
Palleter 40
Tel: 96 382 48 57
Close by the Torres de Cuart, this is one of
the city's most varied Italian restaurants,
with a long wine list and a good lunchtime
menu. Popular with families. Booking rec-
ommended. **€–€€**

Seu-Xerea
Comte Almodóvar 4
Tel: 96 392 40 00
Stephen Anderson's fusion style mixes Oriental with Mediterranean flavours – as in
tuna with *teryaki* and fruit *gazpacho*. Good-
value tasting menu. Summer terrace. **€€**

Sushi Cru
Pintor Zariñena 3
Tel: 96 392 54 92
A great sushi bar with a cosmopolitan staff
and hip clientele. Handily close to IVAM.
No cards. Dinner only in August. **€**

L'Eixample

In the 19th-century grid of streets south of
the old town are smart business and gourmet
restaurants with a mix of local and international flavours.

Albacar
Sorní 35
Tel: 96 395 10 05
Tito Albacar's creative Mediterranean cook-
ing draws a mixed business and gourmet

eft: wine and tapas at the counter

crowd. Dishes include red mullet with sea-urchin vinegar. The glass patio overlooks an indoor garden. Excellent wines. €€€

Cantina Peruana
Ciscar 49
Tel: 96 333 65 42
Ceviche (fish and seafood marinated in lime or lemon juice, with onion and peppers), stuffed potatoes, braised lamb, and great *mojito* cocktails give you a taste of Peru's rich cuisine. Good set menu. €€

El Ángel Azul
Conde de Altea 33
Tel: 96 374 56 56
The kitchen draws on the best of Spanish produce for unusual, French-influenced salads, meat and fish dishes. Business clientele at lunch, when there's a good set menu. Occasional jazz and art shows. €€

El Romeral
Gran Vía Marqués del Turia 62
Tel: 96 395 15 17
Market cooking with emblematic dishes such as *all i pebre* (eel in hot peppery sauce), served in an elegant dining room to a mixed business and local crowd. €€€

Gargantúa
Navarro Reverter 18
Tel: 96 334 68 49
The art nouveau décor, baroque music, summer terrace and haute cuisine – such as duck breast with honey vinegar – make this a local favourite. €€

L'Ecospai
Mossén Femenia (Cura Femenia) 2
Tel: 96 333 30 67
Everything is organic – not just vegetables, but also the ham, cheese and wine. There are tapas as well as meals, and a stage for impromptu performances. Open all year. €

Pizzeria Portofino
Ciscar 28
Tel: 96 333 53 33
A very popular restaurant serving pizzas from a wood-fired oven plus pasta, meat and puddings. Young crowd and slightly older couples. Book. €

Puerto and Malva Rosa
The port has wonderful rice restaurants o the beach, and family fish specialist Ca' Sento is fast becoming a gourmet landmark

Antigua Casa Calabuig
Avinguda del Port (Puerto) 336
Tel: 96 331 02 69
Fabulous people-watching at this louche turn-of-the-20th-century bar opposite th port. Open every day 6am–midnight. Menu of the day, great *bocadillos* (filled rolls), fis tapas, *tortillas, aigua de Valencia* and more.

Bodega Casa Montaña
José Benlliure 69
Tel: 96 367 23 14
A relaxed 19th-century *bodega*, with win barrels and décor intact, a seriously goo wine list and excellent produce served a tapas. Worth a trip. €€

Bodega El Labrador
Dr Manuel Candela 58
Tel: 96 372 75 30
Half-way between the river and the port i this busy, authentic *bodega*, one of the city best, with excellent hams and cheeses. €

Ca'n Sento
Méndez Núñez 17
Tel: 96 330 17 75
Michelin-starred, this small family plac has rapidly become one of Spain's top fis restaurants. Mother and son cook old an new dishes. Worth the steep bill. Gourme tasting menu. €€€

La Rosa
Passeig Neptú 70
Tel: 96 371 20 76
Opened in 1925, this beachside restauran serves classic rice dishes. It proudly declare that all the produce is fresh, for which yo pay a premium. Try the sweet potato cake fo dessert. Lunch only in winter. €€€

Monkili
Passeig Neptú 52
Tel: 96 371 00 39
One of the beachfront's most popular ric restaurants – order in advance by phone Lunch only. €€

Right: tapas bar

Turia's North Bank

Close to the river's north bank a growing cluster of the city's top gourmet restaurants cater to residents, businessmen, hotel guests and concert-goers.

Alejandro

Amadeo de Saboya 15
Tel: 96 393 40 46
Young, highly trained, Michelin-starred chef Alejandro serves updated, lightened versions of Valencian dishes in a tastefully smart setting. Excellent value set lunch. Open all year. €€

Marisquería Civera

Lleida (Lérida) 11 and 13
Tel: 93 347 59 17
Prime seafood plus a few traditional local dishes stand out at this top shellfish restaurant a short walk from Torres de Serrans. Pleasant gardens; business and family clientele. Closes early July. €€€

Joaquín Schmidt

Visitació 7
Tel: 96 340 17 10
Creative Mediterranean cooking at a set price – there are three menus on offer. There is a cosmopolitan crowd; worth booking. €€

La Sacristía

Amadeo de Saboya 28
Tel: 96 361 17 58
This is the place to come for something different – in winter a shepherd's game stew plus venison, cold cuts and farmhouse cheeses. €€

Óscar Torrijos

Finlandia 7 bajo
Tel: 96 393 63 00
Tuna fillet with smoked aubergine and pepper ice cream gives a taste of the avant-garde gourmet cuisine here. Sommelier Raquel Torrijos offers wine by the glass from a spectacular cellar, and there is a tapas bar. The original Michelin-starred home of the restaurant, in the Eixample (Dr Sumsi 4, tel: 96 373 29 49), is also excellent. €€€

Zen

Avinguda Pio XII 33
Tel: 96 348 34 39
Classy Asian fusion from two Michelin-starred chefs who moved here from Amsterdam and Paris. Sushi and lacquered duck are specialities. Open every day of the year. €€€

Tapas

Tapas come in three sizes: *pinchos* (mouthfuls), *tapas* (enough to fill a saucer), and *raciones* (small platefuls). You can usually check out the quality from the dishes laid out on the counters. Local specialities include roasted red peppers and salt cod, squid, braised broad beans and paella.

Classic addresses for each quarter include, in El Carmen, **Café Bar Pilar**, **Ca'n Bermell** *(see page 69)* and **Santa Companya**, Roteros 21. Behind the Town Hall try **Amorós**, En Llop 3. In El Mercat, by the Llotja, try street bars at the **Mercat Central** and **Escalones de La Llotja**, Pere Compte 3. In Cabanyal visit **Bodegas Montaña** and **Antigua Casa Calabuig** *(see page 70)*.

NIGHTLIFE

Hedonistic Valencia parties as if there is no tomorrow. *Guía Azul*, a Spanish guide book, describes it this way: '…you can spend Friday to Monday going without a break from one place to the next, each one of them competing to be the last to close.' On the whole the clubs get lively from 1am or later and keep going till 6–7am, but look carefully and there is indeed 24-hour weekend partying. Then, from Sunday, most places close for two or three nights. Some places also shut in August. The free English-language listings magazine, *24/7*, is especially good on the latest places to go.

Valencia also has a busy cultural life that is keen to compete with that of Madrid and Barcelona. Cinema, theatre, jazz and classical music are the city's strongest suits. The long-delayed addition of the Palau de les Arts, open from 2006, brings opera to the city for the first time. It also aims to offer big international names from every area of music, from pop to baroque opera.

The best way to track down what's on is to buy a daily newspaper or the latest edition of *Cartelera Turia*, the city's weekly listings magazine, which contains a 'Cartela

de Actos Culturales'. Tickets for many events are sold at El Corte Inglés and FNAC *(see Shopping)* and by the internet or phone via Servientrada (tel: 96 399 55 77) and Bancaja (tel: 90 211 55 77).

Bars, Nightclubs and Discos

The night scene is clustered in half a dozen zones. The old town, focused on El Carme (Barrio del Carmen), with the Plaça del Tossal as its epicentre, is the hippest, arty, bohemian gay quarter. In summer, people move out to the River Turia's north bank and the beach area, now less fizzy than it was, but still a lot of fun in the hot months. In the Eixample (Ensanche), in between, are upmarket Plaça de Canóvas del Castillo, Juan Llorens and Avinguda d'Aragó.

Old-town bar-cafés for a first drink range from Café del Negrito (Plaça del Negret/del Negrito), which has a great open-air setting, to Café Lisboa (Plaça Dr Collado, by the Llotja), a laid-back day and night-time café, and Ghecko, done up in Balinese style (Calatrava 10), to Xino Xano (Alta 28), a relaxing club run by a local DJ Xino, open from 3pm. Bosería (Bosería 41), with DJs and good music, offers a designer setting and people-watching for over 25s plus a summer terrace.

Two interesting hybrids of culture-and-fun are Ca'n Revuelta (Santa Teresa 10), an alternative bar-theatre and exhibition space; and Radio City (Santa Teresa 19), a bar with live music and a packed dance floor at weekends, plus a bit of theatre and film thrown in at times. At the other end of the scale La Marxa (Cuines/Cocinas 5), a loud mainstream nightclub, is very popular with younger tourists.

In the summer you can linger over a drink at the fashionable **open-air terraces**, such as Café Valencia and Café el Llebeig, along the breezy Passeig de L'Albereda/Paseo de la Alameda. By the **beach** try Flamingo (Isabel de Villena 57), where you can have a cocktail or ice cream and watch the waves roll in – later there is all-night clubbing here.

Some of the best and most varied **dance floors** are out in the **Eixample** – Gran Café Canovas (Gran Vía Marqués del Turia 76) is long established and still lively, and open from early till late (6pm–3am); Havana (Juan

Above: Café de Madrid, where *Aigüa de Valencia* was created

orens 43), the city's best salsa club, opens 1.30pm–6.30am; and Jam Disclub, behind he railway station (Cuba 8), is the top venue or pan-European dance and electronic rooves. La Indiana (Sant Vicent Martír 97), vith a live shark tank, is a dress-to-impress isco for the bronzed, wealthy local tribe. prize for the best named disco must go to 9 Monos Sobre un Cable de Acero (Eduard oscà 27, tel: 96 337 08 30) – 69 Monkeys n a Steel Wire; open till 6am, it has occa-ional live music.

Opera, Concerts and Other Live Music

he city's flagship venue is the Ciutat de es Arts i Ciències' brand new **Palau de les Arts**, which has four main stages – two of hem able to accommodate audiences of ,800 and the other two with a capacity of 00 each. The Palau's all-encompassing pro-ramme runs from chamber music to con-emporary dance, plus educational activities. vents include a festival coordinated by ubin Mehta and Operalia, an opera com-etition founded by Placido Domingo.

Just a stone's throw up the riverbed is the **alau de la Música** (Passeig de L'Albereda/ aseo de la Alameda 30, tel: 96 337 50 20). t opened in 1987, has two main auditori-ms, which are famed for their acoustics, nd hosts year-round performances of clas-ical music and jazz, plus big names from amenco and pop.

El Loco (Erudit Orellana 12, tel: 96 326 5 26) has daily live blues, rock, fusion, jazz, thnic and rock. There are weekly concerts y established jazz names at **La Linterna** Llanterna/Linterna 11, tel: 96 352 01 61) n the old town. For jazz, blues, soul and unk drop by **Black Note** (Polo y Peyrolón 5, tel: 96 393 36 63).

For flamenco, aim for the **Café del Duende** (Turia 62, tel: 630 45 52 89) on hursday night at 11pm; or **Radio City** on uesday night at 11pm. For indie sounds try **Wah-Wah** (Campoamor 52, tel: 96 356 39 2). **Barracabar** (Jacinto Benavente 5, tel: 6 382 62 22) has late-night concerts, Thurs-ay to Saturday, featuring alternative groups. eatre El Musical (Plaça del Rosario 3, tel: 0 201 24 70) has a mix of theatre and music, uch as the June flamenco festival.

Theatre and Dance

The city often offers a dozen or more pro-ductions at any one time, with cosmopolitan programming. Most performances are given in Spanish or Valencian. The **Teatro Principal** (Barques/Barcas 15, tel: 96 353 92 00), **Teatre Talia** (Cavallers 31, tel: 96 391 50 80) and **L'Altre Espai** (Platero Suárez 11, tel: 96 365 49 20) are the main dance venues for classical, contemporary or staged fla-menco dance. **Sagunt A Escena**, during the summer months, offers concerts and performances by international artists. Infor-mation and tickets for all venues may be obtained via www.teatresgv.com.

Cinemas

Valencia has three cinemas with subtitled original-language films. They are: **Albatros** (Plaça Fra Luis Colómer 4, tel: 96 393 2677), **Babel** (Vicent Sancho Telo 10, tel: 96 362 67 95), and the **Filmoteca** (Plaça del Ajun-tament 17, tel: 96 399 55 77), which has very good old and new programming and open-air summer screenings next to the Palau de la Música. Prices are reasonable.

Casino

Casino Monte Picayo (7pm–4am; entrance €4 or free if you dine there) is next door to luxury hotel Monte Picayo in Puzol (off the motorway A-7, Salida/Exit 7), 14 km (8 miles) from Valencia. It offers American and French roulette, blackjack and slot machines. Dress smartly.

The Gay Scene

Valencia has a thriving gay scene, with restaurants and bars as well as clubs. **Librería Cobertizo** (Plaça Vicente Iborra 4), at the heart of the old town's gay area, is a meet-ing place and general information base. **Sant Miquel** is very elegant and cool, with a large terrace in summer (Plaça Sant Miquel 13) and **Café de la Seu** (Sant Calze 7) is pleas-antly arty. Late at night the best-known venue is **Venial** (Cuarte 26), which has shows, DJs and very late closing.

There is also mainstream music and fun at the **North Dakota Saloon** (Plaça Mar-garita Valldaura 1) and **Discobar La Goulue** (Cuarte 32), and techno and house at **La Guerra** (Cuarte 47).

CALENDAR OF EVENTS

January

Cabalgata de Reyes Magos: On 5 January, the eve of Epiphany, the Three Kings arrive at the city's port at 5pm and parade through the city's streets in carriages before being hoisted up to the town hall balcony in a basket. Here they give every child who visits them a toy. Bakers' windows fill with bread 'crowns' containing lucky charms.

San Antón: The annual blessing of the animals takes place at San Antón church (Carrer Sagunto) on 17 January.

Sant Vicent Màrtir: A morning procession from the cathedral celebrates the feast day (22 January) of the city's patron saint, an early Christian martyr. Another procession to San Esteve church, in 16th-century dress, marks the baptism of Sant Vicent Ferrer.

March

Las Fallas de San José: *Fallas*, the city's main fiesta, is one of the largest in Spain – and certainly the noisiest, filling the streets with lights, processions, fireworks, gunpowder and firecracker displays and huge crowds. It runs in mid-March. An estimated 2 million tourists are said to have visited the *fallas* in 2008. (Note that it is not to everybody's taste – the streets become chaotic and many local people leave the city.) The fiesta grew out of medieval bonfires celebrating the feast-day of St Joseph, the patron saint of carpenters. Satirical, straw-stuffed guys *(ninots)* began to be burned in the 18th century. Today, the guys have grown into huge Disney-style cardboard and resin sculptures, which are erected in squares by each quarter's *falleros* societies. The fiestas themselves have grown into larger week-long celebrations, which include processions, firework displays, children's *fallas* and a two-day floral offering at the Real Basílica de la Mare de Déu de Desamparats (17 and 18 March, 4pm–midnight). On 19 March, the fiestas reach their climax with the *Nit del Foc* – or night of fire. Most *ninots* are burned at midnight, although the giant one in the Plaça del Ajuntament burns an hour later, at 1am, and the children's ones are burned at 8pm. Each year the best *falla* is 'pardoned' and earns itself a place in the Museu Faller, Plaza de Monteolivete 4. Bu... fights are also held every day during the fies...

Easter

Holy Week processions: The processions the city's seaside quarters include 27 brothe... hoods and 5,000 costumed penitents. Be... known are Holy Thursday's silent proce... sion at midnight and the 6.30pm processio... on Good Friday, both starting in Malva Ros... At midnight on Palm Sunday, fireworks ce... ebrate the Resurrection.

Sant Vicent Ferrer: On the Monday aft... Easter, short liturgical plays re-enact the mi... acles of Sant Vicent Ferrer on open-air alta... near his birthplace and elsewhere.

May

La Mare de Déu dels Desamparats: O... the second Sunday in May Valencia pa... homage to the tiny Virgin of the Forsake... who is processed from her home in the bas... ica, next to the cathedral, to be fêted wi... flowers and music. In the Plaça de la Ma... de Déu is a lively ceramics fair.

June

Corpus Christi: Mid- to late June. Today... street processions, first celebrated in 135... originated in the 15th–16th century and kee... their original music, dances, *rocas* – painte... wagons – and characters. The Mom... dressed in white, symbolises virtue co... fronting the Momos, black and yellow dev... like dragon figures. The main procession, th... Cabalgata de la Degolla, usually starts fro... the Plaça de Manises, and the plays are pe... formed in the Plaça de la Mare de Déu.

Nuit de Sant Joan: Revived midsumm... bonfires on 24 June on Malva Rosa beach a... accompanied by wishes for the coming ye... – you wash your feet in the sea and make... wish for the coming year, as the seven... wave breaks over your legs.

August

El Palmar pilgrimage: Held in El Palm... on the first Sunday in August. A crucif... from the church is ferried around Albufe... lake and the fiesta ends with fireworks.

Cristo de la Salud: In El Palmar, the lak... is blessed from a fleet of fishing boats... sunset on 4–6 August.

a Tomatina: The famous tomato-throwing esta held in Bunyol, west of Valencia, sually on the final Wednesday of August, ttracts thousands of visitors.

October

ía de la Comunitat Valenciana: 9 Octo-er, the day that Jaime I took Valencia 1238, is a public holiday celebrating the -gion's 'liberation'. At midnight the city's xpert firework-makers première their new esigns in the spectacular riverbed Festival e Pirotecnica.

Arts and Cultural Festivals

April

ansa València: The Teatre Talia hosts an xcellent contemporary 10-day dance fes-val towards the end of the month.

une–July

estival Eclectíc: An eclectic series of inter-ational stars give concerts against the back-rop of the Ciutat de les Arts i Ciències.

uly

eria de Juli: A month of open-air concerts, eatre performances, a jazz festival, fire-ork displays, bullfights and the Certamen nternacional de Bandas de Música, a long-stablished international competition for unicipal bands. The majority of events are eld in the Jardins del Reial and Passeig de L'Albereda, on the river's north bank. The fair ends with a Battle of Flowers.

Bienal de València: A new event brings together art and architectural projects.

Campus Party: Said to be the world's biggest IT party. Over 100,000 internet enthusiasts get together in the second half of the month to surf, chat and play on-line for 24 hours a day in the City of the Arts and Sciences (www.campus-party.org).

July–August

Festival Internacional de Benicàssim (FIB): Spain's flagship open-air rock and indie music festival, held in this seaside town to the north of Valencia in late July/early August, is now one of Europe's best-known.

July–September

La Filmoteca d'Estiu: Open-air film festi-val in the gardens of the Palau de la Música.

September

Feria Internacional del Mueble: The Inter-national Furniture Fair held in the trade fair-ground in early September is one of Europe's most important furniture-design events.

October

Iberflora: Spain's most notable plant-and-flower show, expanding all the time, is held in the trade fairground.

Mostra de Cine del Mediterrani: this month-long festival of Mediterranean cin-ema is centred at the Filmoteca.

bove: La Nit del Foc; *fallas* bonfires

Practical
Information

GETTING THERE

By Air

Valencia's airport, Manises, is 8km (5 miles) west of the city limits on the N-220, off the A-3 (information, tel: 96 159 85 00/96 159 85 5). Iberia-Air Nostrum, Vueling, Spainair and Air Europa operate domestic flights from 7 Spanish airports. Iberia, British Airways, easyJet, Air France, Ryanair, Alitalia, Portualia and Thomsonfly operate from 24 European airports. There are also flights from North Africa, eastern Europe and Turkey. The Spanish airline, Iberia, operates direct flights to Valencia from North America.

The journey to and from the airport may be made by bus or taxi. There is a direct airport bus, Aero-Bus, which runs every 20 minutes, 6am–10pm, and costs €2.50. The bus stops at the airport (departures terminal), Avda del Cid (police office), St Bailén, the junction of Angel Guimerá and Juan Llorens, Avda del Cid and the airport (departures terminal). Alternatively, take the yellow No 150 city bus, which runs every 15 minutes, 5.20am–11pm, and leaves you in the Plaça de España, close to the central train station. For the return journey Line 150 buses leave from the Central Bus Station. The journey takes 45 minutes and costs €1 (information, tel: 96 150 70 82). Taxis cost around €14, with a supplement for large luggage and a small increase after 10pm and on Sundays.

A metro link to the city centre leaves from the new terminal for domestic flights. It takes around 20 minutes to reach the town centre on the L5 line.

By Rail

The main RENFE train station is Estació del Nord (Xátiva 24). Direct mainline trains arrive from Madrid (3½ hours in the Alarís), Alicante (1½ hours in the Euromed) and Barcelona (3½ hours in the Euromed). A high-speed train will also connect Valencia with Alicante and Madrid from 2009.

Left: La Peinata. **Right:** tiled frieze, Casa-Museu Benlliure

Station facilities include left-luggage lockers with 24-hour access, taxis, car rental, shops, cash machines and tourist information. There are no facilities for changing money. Disabled travellers can request help at Atención al Cliente. Tickets can be bought at train stations, RENFE offices and authorised travel agencies any time from 60 days prior to departure. Some travel agencies charge an additional fee. Tickets may also be bought by telephone or via the RENFE website (www. renfe.es). Children under four travel free; those aged four to eleven have a 40 percent discount. Return tickets have a 20 percent discount. Information and tickets, tel: 90 224 02 02.

By Road

Valencia is 502km (311 miles) from the French border on the A-7 motorway (tolled), and 350 km (218 miles) from Madrid on the A-3 motorway (untolled). A car is not needed in the city and is even a hindrance. 24-hour help is available from RACE (General Aviles 64, tel: 90 212 04 41). Traffic information may be found on www.valencia.es.

Coach links to Valencia from Madrid, Barcelona, Seville and other cities arrive at the Estació Central de Autobuses, Avda Menéndez Pidal 13 (tel: 96 346 62 66), on the river's right bank. It has a taxi rank and bus links around the city and is also on the metro network. The main long-distance coach operator for the city is Alsa/Enatcar (tel: 90 242 22 42 or 91 754 20 04 and www.alsa.es).

Speed limits are clearly marked (120km/75 miles on motorways, 110km/69 miles on highways and 50km/31 miles in town). They are fully enforced, sometimes with cameras.

CASA·MUSEO BENLLIURE

By Sea

Transmediterranea (tel: 90 245 46 45 and www.transmediterranea.com) runs car and passenger ferry services from Valencia port to Ibiza, Mallorca and Menorca.

TRAVEL ESSENTIALS

When to Visit

Valencia's climate is mild and humid around the year, with temperatures averaging 20°C (68°F). In spring and autumn both the days and evenings are comfortably warm. In the city's mid-March fiestas, *fallas*, the city packs out with visitors and hotel prices hit their peak. Summers are sweltering. Many family businesses close in August. The sea temperature is ideal for bathing from May to October.

Visas and Passports

EU nationals require only a national identity card. All other non-Spanish nationals require passports and may require tourist visas (check this with your nearest Spanish Embassy). These are valid for 90 days and can be renewed once within each one-year period, from outside Spain. Longer stays for non-EU nationals require a resident's card. It is sensible to carry photocopies of your passport with you as ID in case of emergencies, but you need the original to check in at hotels.

Customs

Declarations at customs are not usually necessary if you are arriving in Spain from another country with the EU. Visitors can carry up to €6,000 in cash without declaring it. Limits for alcohol and tobacco follow EU regulations. To get sales-tax-refund invoices stamped, you need to go the Guardia Civil at Manises airport (tel: 96 367 13 00).

Weather

Valencia's mild climate is characterised by year-round sunshine, high humidity and low rainfall, mainly between January and April. July and August are hot; temperatures reach 35°C (95°F) regularly and accommodation with air conditioning is advisable. January to March are the coolest months, when temperatures range from 7 to 17°C (44–63°F).

Clothing

A warm jumper and jacket are useful in winter. In summer light clothes made from natural fibres are preferable. Sunglasses are essential if you are outside a lot. Beach clothes are not usually worn in the town centre, and you need to cover up in churches.

Electricity

Plugs have two round pins. Voltage is 220 AC. Convertors and/or adaptor plugs for electrical appliances are easily purchased at airports.

Time Differences

Spain is one hour ahead of Greenwich Mean Time (GMT). In January the sun rises at about 8.15am and sets at about 6pm; the corresponding times in June are 5.45am and 8.15pm, although the light lingers for another two hours. The clock goes forward in March and back in October, in line with other EU countries.

GETTING ACQUAINTED

Geography

Valencia, Spain's third city, with an estimated population of 791,000 people, sit on Spain's Mediterranean eastern coastal plain. The River Turia around which the city grew has been diverted south to avoid flooding. Industrial and residential suburb have overgrown the city's fertile market gardens, but citrus groves flourish behind the sandy beaches running north and south.

Valencia's port is growing considerably and its waterfront is being greened and opened to the public.

Government and Economy

Spain is a parliamentary democracy ruled by King Juan Carlos I de Borbón since 197, and governed by the socialists (PSOE) since March 2004. However, Valencia's regional and city government are currently in the hands of the conservative party (PP).

Language

Valencia has been a bilingual city since 1982 Valencian – very similar or, according to some linguists, identical to Catalan –

understood by 70 percent of residents. It is increasingly the written and spoken language of local government as well as regional television, radio, road signs, political graffiti and arts performances. However, Spanish (*castellano*) is spoken by nearly everybody in the city.

Religion

Roman Catholicism is Spain's official religion, although fewer than 25 percent of Spaniards go to church regularly. Anglican and Evangelical churches have services in English. The church of San Juan del Hospital, Trinquet de Cavallers 5 (tel: 96 392 29 65) holds English-language mass at noon on Saturdays. The city's synagogue is at Uruguay 59, floor 13 (tel: 96 334 34 16), and the mosque is at the Centro Cultural Islamica, Mendes Núñez 47 (tel: 96 360 33 30).

How Not to Offend

In general, Spaniards have an easygoing but genuine courtesy based on consideration as much as etiquette, but they can be defensive when they feel they are being criticised or laughed at by foreigners. Older Spaniards, or those in formal positions, may expect you to use the formal *usted* rather than *tu* for you'. Wearing skimpy beach clothes in city centres is frowned upon, especially in places of worship.

Population and Ethnicity

Valencia city's population stands at 791,000 while that of the region totals 1.8 million. It has long been one of Spain's most ethnically varied cities thanks to its port. Industrialisation has attracted migration from North Africa and, more recently, from Latin America and eastern Europe. To the south of the city are resorts where northern Europeans, most of them retired, make up 10–25 percent of the population.

MONEY MATTERS

Currency

The currency of Spain is the euro (€), which comes in coins of 1, 2, 5, 10, 20 and 50 centimos, plus 1 and 2 euros. Notes are worth 5, 10, 20, 50, 100, 200 and 500 euros.

Credit Cards and Cash Machines

Many hotels, upmarket restaurants, all department stores, petrol stations, railway and bus stations accept credit-card payment, provided you can offer accompanying ID with a photo. Visa and Mastercard are the most widely accepted cards.

Using your Personal Identification Number (PIN), you can withdraw cash from many 24-hour dispensers *(caixeros/cajeros)*. Note that some savings banks' dispensers will not accept foreign cards. The exchange rate

Above: the Port Authority building

used is printed on your receipt. Numbers for lost or stolen credit cards are as follows: Amex, tel: 90 099 44 26; Diners Club, tel: 91 701 59 00; Mastercard, tel: 90 097 12 31; Visa, tel: 90 099 12 16.

Tipping

Service is included in bills, but it is usual to tip in bars and restaurants, taxis, hotels, cloakrooms and hairdressing salons. Tourist guides may also expect a tip. The size of the tip can vary; from 5–10 percent in a restaurant to 2–3 percent in a taxi, depending on the spare change you have. Note that it is considered offensive to give too small a tip rather than none.

Taxes

Sales tax, called IVA, varies from 7 percent in cafés, restaurants and hotels to 16 percent on certain shop purchases. It is generally included in menu prices, but not quoted in hotel costs. Non-EU residents can reclaim IVA paid on purchases over €90.15, if the receipts are stamped when leaving Spain *(see Customs, page 78)*.

Changing Money

The sign *Cambi/Cambio* (exchange) indicates that a bank offers the service. Banks are open Mon–Fri 8.30am or 9am–2 or 2.30pm. Some banks open Saturday 8.30 or 9am–1pm. Outside these hours, you can change money at bureau (there is one at the airport). Check the commission charage and the exchange rate first. In all cases you will need your passport.

GETTING AROUND

Most sights lie within walking distance in the city centre. There is very little public transport – either buses or metro – in the old town. Buses, the metro, the tram or taxis work well for longer journeys. The No 5 bus, which circles the old town, is very useful for sightseeing. A car is helpful, but not vital, for excursions outside the city.

Taxis

Taxis are good for getting around the city. An available taxi displays either a green light or a sign saying *Llibre*. The meter should be running. Surcharges are added to the basic fare late at night (11pm to 6am), on Sundays and public holidays, for trips outside the city and to the airport, for pickups from taxi ranks and for luggage. Tipping of 2–3 percent is expected. 24 hour telephone taxi services are Teletaxi, tel: 96 357

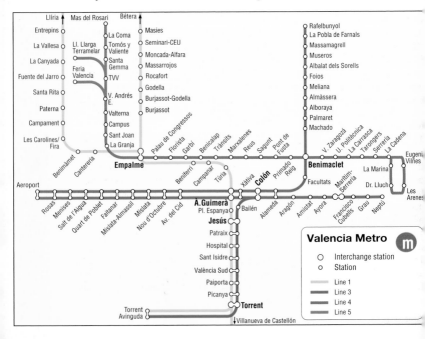

13 13, Radio Taxi, tel: 96 370 33 33 and Valencia Taxi, tel: 96 374 02 02.

Trains

Valencia's main station is Estació del Nord, Xátiva 24 (tel: 90 224 02 02), 10 minutes walk from the Plaça del Ajuntament.

Regional trains run by RENFE, the Spanish railway network, vary in price and speed from the fast Talgo to the slow Regional Exprés and Regional. A train's category is shown on the departures board. The main local lines run to Gandia (C-1, south down the coast past Cullera and Sueca), Castelló de la Plana (C-6, north up the coast via Puig and Sagunt), Utiel (C-3, via Bunyol and Requena), Moixent (C-2, via Xativa), and Riba-Roja de Turia (C-4, via Manises).

Some trains pass through a second station, Cabanyal, usefully close to the port and beach area, on Avda Blasco Ibáñez.

Metro, Tram and Bus

The same flat-price tickets are used for bus, metro and tram. Both metros and trams run from 5.30am–midnight. You can buy single tickets (€1) on the spot, but a B-10 ten-ride *bono* (€5.50), sold at stationers and newspaper shops, is better value. Valencia Card offers unlimited travel on all metros, buses and trams together with museum and shop discounts for one or three days (tel: 90 070 18 18). Prices are: 1 day €6, 2 days €10 and 3 days €12. There is a one-month pass for unlimited travel, which includes local trains, called Abona Zona A, sold at metro and train stations.

Metro Valencia (tel: 96 397 65 65) has four lines (L1, L3, L4 and L5), mainly serving the suburbs and dormitory villages and towns and is expanding rapidly. Useful central stations are Xátiva (L3 and L5), by the railway station, Angel Guimera (L1, L3, L5), Pont de Fusta (L4) and Alameda, in the riverbed, closest to the City of Arts and Sciences (L3).

The electric tram (T4), which you can catch from Pont de Fusta on the river's north bank, links the city centre to the port and the beach quarters. L5 has been extended to link the airport to the city and port.

Extensions currently being built include T2, which will connect the town centre (Xátiva and the old town) to the City of Arts and Sciences; T6, the circular Orbital, which will link the bus station, City of Arts and Sciences and other mid-town locations; and T8, which will connect the airport to towns to the south.

The city has 91 bus routes. Most run from 5.30am to 10.30pm. Seven night-bus routes radiate out from the Plaça del Ajuntament, running every 45 minutes until 3am Thur–Sat, and until 1am Sun–Wed. In the summer three extra buses, the 20, 21 and 22, link the city centre with the port and beach. Information: tel: 96 380 31 82 or 96 352 83 99; www.emtvalencia.es.

Buses for destinations elsewhere in the province are yellow. Destinations include Sagunt, Requena, El Saler and Xàtiva. They

Above: Estació del Nord

leave from the Estació Central de Autobuses, Avda Menendez Pidal. For information and timetables, tel: 96 346 62 66.

Car Rental

To rent a car in Spain you must be at least 19 years of age, and a holder of either an international driving licence or a valid licence with ID photos from your own country. You will also need to show your passport or ID card. Payment is required via a major credit card unless you leave a large cash deposit. You are also obliged to take out insurance.

Cars can be rented per day with an extra payment for mileage, or in package deals for a set number of days with unlimited mileage. Check whether IVA (VAT) is included in the quoted price. It is always cheaper to replace the used petrol yourself. Car hire (Avis tel: 96 152 21 62, Hertz tel: 90 240 24 05, Europcar tel: 90 210 50 30) is available at the airport or at the central railway station (Avis, Europcar and National-Atesa, tel: 96 351 71 45).

Bicycle Rental

Valencia is flat, and there are new cycle lanes in many areas of the city, along the beach and in the nearby countryside. You can also take bicycles free on the metro. They can be hired from Orange Bikes (Sta Teresa 8, tel: 96 391 75 51, www.orangebikes.net), Valencia Bikes (Pg de la Petxina 32, tel: 96 385 17 40, www.valenciabikes.com). Helmets and locks are provided. Rates are around €12–15 a day. Ecotours Cycles, found in the riverbed, next to the Parc de Gulliver, rent bikes and pedal buggies to use in the river's park.

HOURS AND HOLIDAYS

Business Hours

A growing number of small and large shops are open all day, usually 10am to 9pm, but most businesses, both offices and shops, are open Monday to Friday/Saturday from 9 or 10am to 2pm and from 5 to 8pm. Between June and September many businesses work Monday to Friday from 8 or 9am to 3pm, and close in August. Municipal markets usually open by 8.30am and close between 2 and 3pm. In the evening, restaurant hours are later than in many countries: usually 1 to 4pm and 9 to 11.30pm. Most museums are closed all day Monday.

Public Holidays

The following dates are national public holidays: 1 Jan (New Year's Day), 6 Jan (Epiphany, called the Three Kings), Maundy Thursday, Good Friday, 1 May (Labour Day), Corpus Christi (late May or early June), 25 July (St James' Day), 15 Aug (Assumption) 12 Oct (Columbus Day, 1 Nov (All Saints' Day), 6 Dec (Constitution Day), 8 Dec (Immaculate Conception), 25 Dec (Christmas). Local holidays are 22 Jan (Sant Vicent Martír), 19 Mar (St Joseph), the Monday following Easter week (Sant Vicent Ferrer) and 9 Oct (Día de la Comunitat Autonoma).

ACCOMMODATION

Valencia has three main hotel areas. The historic old town and neighbouring commercial quarter, around the Plaça del Ajuntament offers the widest choice. Here you can choose between pensions, hostels, boutique or historic hotels ranging from €14 to over €170

Above: a shop in Plaça de Dóctor Collado

night for a double room. Noise levels, expensive car parks and lack of air conditioning in budget accommodation can be drawbacks.

second cluster of upmarket highrise hotels along the river's north bank are handily close to the Ciutat de les Arts i les Ciències and the river's parks and gardens, but less well placed for historic sights and nightlife. The third area, the Port and beach, combines old-fashioned seaside hostels and stylish new hotels opened for the America's Cup.

High-season prices run from mid-July to early September, and cover Christmas, Easter and the mid-March *Fallas* fiesta fortnight, when central room prices can double and booking is necessary well ahead.

Some business-oriented hotels have excellent weekend offers in summer.

Prices are coded as follows: **€** = under €55; **€€** = €55–100; **€€€** = €100–150; **€€€€** = over €150.

The stars shown indicate each hotel's official international rating.

Ciutat Vella (Old Town)

Ad Hoc ★★★
Boix 4
Tel: 96 391 91 40. Fax: 96 391 36 67
www.adhochoteles.com
small 19th-century hotel in the Barri del Carme, near the river, with stylish rooms en suite and an excellent, if pricey, restaurant. Book ahead. **€€€**

Antigua Morellana ★
En Bou 2
Tel: 96 391 57 73. Fax: 96 391 59 79
www.hostalam.com
friendly family-run hostel close to the market in El Carme, inside an 18th-century building, with plain modern bedrooms with bath and TV. Good value. **€**

Astoria Palace ★★★★
Plaça Rodrigo Botet 5
Tel: 96 398 10 00. Fax: 96 398 10 10
www.hotel-astoria-palace.com
Classic luxury hotel in a small square just outside the old town, with excellent service, rooftop garden and a good restaurant. The bar is a popular local meeting place. Booking essential. Public parking only. **€€€**

El Rincón ★
Cardá 11
Tel: 96 391 79 98/391 60 83
Very clean, extremely cheap, good-value hostel-pension close to the central market. Some of the rooms have bathrooms, heating and air conditioning. Unusually, it has a garage. **€**

Hilux Hostel ★
Calle Cadirers 11
Tel: 96 391 46 91
www.likeathome.net
Ten designer rooms share four bathrooms at this hip travellers' hostel in El Carme. Washing machines, bike hire, kitchen access, DVDs and luggage storage on offer. **€**

Jardín Botanico ★★★★
Dr Peset Cevera 6
Tel: 96 315 40 12. Fax: 96 315 34 08
www.hoteljardinbotanico.com
An elegant townhouse hotel just outside the old town, next to the botanical garden. The rooms have hydromassage and stereo. Breakfast and room-service food. There's also a garage. **€€€**

Plaça del Ajuntament & Around

Continental ★★
Correu 8
Tel: 96 353 52 82. Fax: 96 353 11 13
www.contitel.es
Classically furnished hotel with comfy rooms and cheerful modern Mediterranean décor. Public parking close by. Breakfast included. **€€**

Londres ★★★
Barcelonina 1
Tel: 96 351 22 44. Fax: 96 352 15 08
Choose the top floors of this good-value family hotel for splendid views over the city's main square. The breakfast area boasts a small terrace. Rooms vary in size. **€€**

Melia Inglés Boutique Hotel ★★★
Marqués de Dos Aigües 6
Tel: 96 351 64 26. Fax: 96 394 02 51
www.sh-hoteles.com
Once an urban palace, now a characterful hotel with a few rooms claiming a view over the splendid neighbouring palace. The café-bar and restaurant are popular with locals. **€€€**

Meliá Plaza ★★★★
Plaça del Ajuntament 4
Tel: 96 352 06 12. Fax: 96 352 04 26
www.solmelia.es
Very central, if less than stylish, hotel with
excellent facilities – gym, sauna, garden-
terrace, restaurant and garage. €€€

Moratín ★
Moratín 15
Tel/fax: 96 352 12 20
E-mail: info@hmoratin.com
Tucked away on a side street close to the
Plaça del Ajuntament, this family-owned
hostel has quiet rooms split between two
floors. No air conditioning. Breakfast on
offer. €

Palau de la Mar ★★★★★
Navarro Reverter 14–16
Tel: 96 316 28 84. Fax: 96 316 28 85
E-mail: palaudemar@hospes.es
The city centre's new five-star hotel is built
within two 19th-century urban palaces – the
interior patio sets the tone. Excellent restau-
rant. €€€

Petit Palace Bristol ★★★
Abadía de San Martí 3
Tel: 96 394 51 00. Fax: 96 394 38 50
www.bristol@hthoteles.com
Chic designer hotel in a pedestrian alley

between smart shopping streets. Choos
between high-tech, family and executiv
rooms. Breakfasts are served in the multi
purpose café-bar. €€€€

Reina Victoria ★★★★
Barques (Barcas) 4
Tel: 96 352 04 87. Fax: 96 352 27 21
www.husa.es
Recently refurbished from top to bottom
this belle-époque hotel with a stunning a
deco salon is a good central choice. Plai
bedrooms. Limited parking. €€€

Sorolla ★★★
Convent de Santa Clara 5
Tel: 96 352 33 92. Fax: 96 352 14 65
www.hotelsorolla.com
A stone's throw from the railway statior
completely refurbished in 2002, with som
soundproofed family rooms. Buffet break
fast in the price. €€€

Venecia ★★
En Llop 5
Tel: 96 352 42 67. Fax: 96 352 44 21
www.hotelvenecia.com
Simple but comfortable, with Mediterranea
décor, this hostel has a splendid roof terrac
overlooking the main Plaça del Ajuntament
Breakfast only. All rooms have interne
access. €€

River's North Bank
Cónsul del Mar ★★★★
Avinguda del Port (Puerto) 39
Tel: 96 362 54 32. Fax: 96 362 16 25
www.hotelconsuldelmar.com
Housed in a graceful old consulate build
ing, the hotel has easy access to the port an
the City of Arts and Sciences, a small indoo
pool and private parking. Weekend deals ar
available. €€€

Holiday Inn Express Ciudad de Las Ciencias ★★★
Escriptor Rafael Ferreres 22
Tel: 96 316 25 30. Fax: 96 395 28 48
www.valencia-ciencies.hiexpress.com
Just 300 metres (985 ft) away from the City c
Arts and Sciences, this newly built hotel wit
private garage and swimming pool is a good
value option for car and family visits. €€

Above: the characterful Melia Inglés *(see page 83)*

H Center ★★★★
icardo Micó 1
l: 96 347 50 00. Fax: 96 347 62 52
ww.nh-hotels.com
he sleek functional décor, restaurants,
orts facilities and speedy service are
eared to businessmen, but are relaxing for
olidaymaking too. Close to the Museum
f Fine Arts, this branch also has a large
arden. Access to public parking. **€€€**

ort

ostal Miramar
g de Neptú 32
el: 96 371 51 42
ww.petitmiramar.com
ld-world small seafront hostel above the
aella restaurants right on the beach. All
ooms with bath. Breakfast included. Prices
ouble in the summer season. **€€**

otel Neptuno
g de Neptú 2
el: 96 35 67 777. Fax: 96 356 0430
ww.hotelneptunovalencia.com
ight on the seafront, this hotel opened in
004 in the run-up to the America's Cup.
ea views and modern creative cooking.
reakfast buffet. **€€€**

H Ciudad de Valencia ★★★
vinguda del Port (Puerto) 214
el: 96 330 75 00. Fax: 96 330 98 64
ww.nh-hotels.com
 modern hotel, situated very close to the
ort, with all the facilities required for busi-
ess or for a holiday stay. There's a good
estaurant, and the hotel has its own car park.
Veekend offers. **€€**

H Atarazanas ★★★
laça Tribunal de los Aigües 4
el: 96 320 30 10. Fax: 96 320 30 15
iscreet, mid-size hotel right behind the
ort with minimalist décor and a glass-
valled restaurant. Rooms are functional.
iood value. **€€**

partments & Self-Catering

ome Backpackers ★★
laça Vicente Iborra s/n
el: 96 391 37 97
ww.likeathome.net

The cheapest hostel rooms in the city, with
kitchen access and good facilities. Also at
La Lonja 4, tel: 96 391 62 29. **€**

Venecia ★★
En Llop 5
Tel: 96 352 42 67. Fax: 96 352 44 21
www.hotelvenecia.com
Self-catering apartments overlooking the
Plaça del Ajuntament. **€€**

Outside the City

Ad Hoc Parque ★★★★
*Crtra San Antonio de Benageber a Betera
km 3*
Tel: 96 169 83 93. Fax: 96 391 36 67
www.adhochoteles.com
This smart new hotel sited opposite the
famed Escorpión golf course and close to
the airport offers good sports and children's
facilities, a garden and an excellent restaurant. Very quiet. **€€€**

Parador de Turismo El Saler
Avinguda de los Pinares 151, El Saler
Tel: 96 161 11 86. Fax: 96 162 70 16
www.saler@parador.es
This beach hotel with sea views sits among
pine-trees – both the Albufera natural park
and world-famous El Saler golf course are
a short walk away. **€€€**

HEALTH & EMERGENCIES

General Health
Water is clean everywhere, but does not
always taste very good. The bottled variety
is cheap to buy and is automatically offered
in bars and restaurants when you order water.
Agua no potable indicates that water should
not be drunk.

Pharmacies
Spanish pharmacists are highly trained
paramedics and can deal with many minor
ailments. Identified by a green or red cross,
*farmacia*s open 9.30am–2pm and 4–8pm on
weekdays, and for the morning hours only
on Saturdays. A list of on-duty pharmacies
providing an emergency service can be
found on the door of each one or you can
ring 90 050 09 52 for the information. The

Farmacia Gran Vía 55, tel: 96 351 22 20) is open 24 hours a day 7 days a week.

Medical/Dental Services

If you are an EU resident and have a European Health Insurance Card (replacing the E111 form from January 2006), obtainable from the Post Office, you are eligible for free treatment from the Spanish national health service. You will need to pay for medicines and, possibly, tests. For extra protection take out medical insurance.

In an emergency, you can make a free call for an ambulance on 112, or ring Red Cross emergencies 96 367 73 75, or go direct to an *ambulatorio* (general day-care outpatient clinic) or emergency department *(urgencias)* at one of the city's hospitals. If you do so, take your European Health Insurance Card with you or, if you do not have one, take a passport. The main hospitals are: in the port and beach area Hospital Clínico (Avda Blasco Ibáñez 17, tel: 96 386 26 00), close to the river Hospital de la Fe (Avda Campanar 21, tel: 96 386 27 00) and, on the western side of town, Hospital General (Avda de las Tres Creus, tel: 96 197 20 00). Vaccinations are not generally needed.

Crime and Police

Take elementary precautions to avoid pickpockets or other theft, especially in petrol stations, bus and train stations, and during fiestas. The police are unlikely to try to find your belongings, but you will need to fill in a form at the local station for insurance purposes. The general emergency line is 112. Other emergency numbers are national police 091, local police 092, civil guard 062.

Central stations include Alt 43 (in the old town, tel: 96 391 76 36), Francesc Cubells 58 (in the port, tel: 96 367 91 12), Avda del Cid 37 (western Eixample: tel: 96 384 00 92) and Gran Vía Ramón y Cajal 40 (near the train station, tel: 96 353 95 39). Drug dealing and trafficking are illegal in Spain.

Toilets

It is general practice to use toilets in bars – buying a coffee as a thank you – and petrol stations. Toilets do not always have paper. In summer blue-flag beaches have portacabin toilets.

Fire

The emergency line is 112.

COMMUNICATIONS & NEWS

Post

The main post office on the Plaça del Ajuntament, has a fax service and telephones (Mon–Fri 8.30am–8.30pm, Sat 9.30am–2pm). The 'poste restante' address is Lista de Correos, Correos Central, 46001 Valencia. Stamps can also be purchased at tobacconists *(estancos)*, which show a 'Tabacos' street sign.

Telephone

Public phone boxes (open blue kiosks) have instructions in English. You can use coins or phone cards, which are sold at newsagents. Some booths take credit cards. There are also large telephone and post offices where calls are paid for after they have been made. You can make a reverse-charge call from these offices or from a call box. Calls are cheaper after 8pm and at weekends. Many bars, hotels, restaurants and petrol stations have coin-operated phones; the fees vary.

The international code for Spain is 34, the area code for Valencia city and province is 96. You need to use this area code at all times even if you are phoning within the city. For directory enquiries within Spain phone 11888 (a fee is charged) or access www.paginas-amarillas.es

For international calls, dial the general access code (00) and the relevant country code (listed in public phone boxes). For international enquiries dial 1025 and to get help from the international operator, tel 1008. Discount cards and public phone shops *(locutorios)* with satellite links offer the cheapest international calls.

Telegrams may be sent by telephone: 96 310 27 66.

Internet Connections

Many hotels have internet access from rooms or from the lobby. Some post offices do too. There is internet access at the airport. Central cybercafés include Ono, Sant Vicent Martír 22, with broadband internet, open

 aily till 1am (www.ono.com). Workcen-
r, Ribera 19, tel: 96 112 08 30, is a more
xpensive 24-hour option with multiple
ork facilities.

Media

he main national newspapers are *El País*
entre-left), *abc* (centre-right) and *El
undo* (neutral). They include regional
ages with local news and listings. Local
ewspapers include *El Levante* (centre-left),
nd *Las Provincias* (centre-right). Inter-
ational newspapers are sold in the large
osks in the centre of town. *Cartelera Turia*,
t up in the 1960s, is the city's much-loved
eekly listings magazine. *24–7* is a monthly
nglish-language equivalent packed with
ood information and opinion pieces. *Marca*,
e country's best-selling newspaper, is for
otball and sports lovers.

USEFUL INFORMATION

nformation Websites

ebsites with useful information include
e following:

ww.barriodelcarmen.net Neighbours'
ebsite for the medieval quarter.

ww.cac.es Ciutat de les Artes i Ciències
te for information and booking.

bove: internet café
ight: kite on the beach

www.canalgv.es Long-distance education
learning site showing programmes made for
Canal 9 television.

www.comunitat-valenciana.com The official regional tourist site.

www.costablanca-news.com Linked to a
weekly paper for expatriates, with local service listings.

www.culturia.org Local cultural life.

www.gva.es The regional government site,
with multiple links.

www.turisvalencia.es A city business and
tourist visitor site.

www.24-7valencia.com English listings
magazine site.

www.valenciaterraimar.org The site for
Valencia province.

www.valenciawebtr.com Locally run food
and travel site.

Disabled

Awareness is increasing, but facilities such
as lifts and adapted toilets are still few in
number. There is access for the disabled
on all buses and trams, and help is provided
at the central train station. NH Center,
Ad Hoc, the Astoria Palace and Consul del
Mar are well-adapted central hotels. Most
public galleries and museums also have
wheelchair access.

Children

Many attractions are designed for children.
L'Oceanogràfic, Museu de les Ciències and
Museu de Ciències Naturals are especially
good, with some English-language information. Parc de Gulliver is a popular riverbed
play area, and there are small play areas on all
blue-flag beaches. The city's main fiesta, *Fallas*, has a children's section. Other visits could
include the Casa de los Caramelos, a large
old sweet shop at Muro de Sta Ana 6; the
Museu del Juguete, in Universitat Politecnica (tel: 96 387 70
30), the Toy Museum;
and, in Cabanyal, the
Teatro de Marionetas La
Estrella at Los Angeles
33, a puppet theatre (tel:
96 356 22 92).

Maps

Basic city maps are available from the tourist offices *(see page 90)*. Librería Regolf, at Mar 22 (tel: 96 392 23 62), has an excellent ranges of maps and guidebooks.

Bookshops

Try Books On Spain – www.books-on-spain.com – for out-of-print and antiquarian works. For general books, try París-València, a classic shop – its oldest branch is at Pelayo 7, next to the train station (tel: 96 352 54 40). FNAC, Guillem de Castro, No 9, and El Corte Inglés in the Mercat de Colom basement also sell guidebooks.

ATTRACTIONS

Valencia has many small specialised museums, most of which are free. The following includes some of the best that are not featured in the main itineraries in this book. Further information is also given on www.xarxamuseus.com.

Antic Monestir de San Miquel dels Reis, Avda de la Constitució 284. Splendid 16th-century building with cloisters and doorway. It was later used as prison and now houses Valencia's main library, with outstanding manuscripts on show (Tues–Fri 10am–2pm, 4.30–8pm, Sat–Sun 10am–2pm; free).

Archivo del Reino de Valencia, Pg de L'Albereda/L'Alameda, tel: 96 360 31 23, and **Biblioteca Historica de la Universitat de Valencia**, tel: 96 386 41 18. Valencian historic archives.

Col.legi de l'Art Major de la Seda, Hospital 7, tel: 96 351 19 51. Fifteenth-century home of the silk-makers' guild, with a fine spiral staircase and tiling. Currently being refurbished; due to reopen in 2009.

Convent de Sant Domènech, Pl de Tetuán 22, tel: 96 196 30 38 from 3–5pm. Once the city's largest monastery, this National Artistic Monument set behind a Renaissance façade is now the police headquarters. Some areas may be visited, including the splendid 15th-century Chapel of the Kings. Other areas – the cloisters, refectory and capitular room, reminiscent of the Llotja – are occupied by the police and can be seen by arrangement only (8.30am–1.30pm; free).

Convent de la Trinitat, Alboraia s/ Fifteenth-century convent with Gothic cloister and church redecorated in baroque time The convent houses the Sala Parpallo, whe prizewinning Parpallo works are exhibite

L'Antiga Universitat, Universitat 2, tel: 9 386 41 00 to arrange visit. Built in the 16th century, although today largely dating fro the mid-19th, with an interesting patio ar changing exhibitions (Mon–Thur; free).

Museu de la Ciutat, Pl del Arquebisbe An 18th–19th century palace housing secondary collection of 15th- to 20th-century Valencian art and another of weigh and measures (Tues–Sat 10am–2pm, 4.30 8.30pm, Sun 10am–3pm; admission fee).

Museu de Prehistòria, Corona 36. Ju round the corner from IVAM, this almshous also known as the Casa de la Benificienci is now home to a regional archaeology ar prehistory museum. Great shop and terrac café (Tues–Sun 10am–8pm; free).

Museu Faller, Pl Montolivet 4. Charmin small museum which contains the winnin *ninot indultado*, or 'pardoned guy' since 193 Track the change from pre-1950s wax, clo and straw figures to today's Disney-sty ones (Tues–Sat 10am–2pm, 4.30–8.30pr Sun and hols 10am–3pm; admission fee).

Museu d'Història de Valencia (MhV) Valè cia 1. Imaginative, child-friendly compute simulations tell the story of the city's histo (Tues–Sat 10am–2pm, 4.30–8.30pm; Sun ar hols 10am–3pm).

MUVIM **(Museo Valencia de la Il.lustraci y la Modernitat)**, Guillem de Castro 8. Goc contemporary exhibitions, plus a wide-scree audiovisual exhibit (book ahead for this) abo the city's history since the enlightenment. Ou side are the Jardins del Antic Hospital, wi their palms and old stones (Tues–Sat 10am 2pm, 4–8pm; Sun 10am–8pm; free).

Palacio de Cervello, Pl de Tetuán 3, tel: 9 352 54 78 ext 4496. The impressive res dence of monarchs and notable figures fro the 19th century.

Palau de Valeriola, Valeriola 13. A bea tifully converted 14th-century palace, whic houses a private collection of contemporar Spanish art built up by two Valencian colle tors. Their foundation also hosts temporar exhibitions (Tues–Sun 10am–2pm, 5–8pm admission fee).

practical information

GUIDED TOURS

Walking tours: A 2-hour walking tour leaves the town hall at 10am on Saturdays (tel: 96 385 17 40). The city also has a *Museo Abierto* scheme, which allows you to phone up for multilingual information outside each signed site. Convenient but pricey.

Bicycle tours: Every Saturday there are guided bicycle tours to the river, old city and City of Arts and Sciences (tel: 96 385 17 40).

Bus tours: The open-topped double-decker Bús Turistic leaves from Pl de la Reina every 20 minutes during the day and offers a 24-hour ticket, stopping at main sights outside the old town (€12 adults, €6 children).

PARKS

Valencia city has wonderful green spaces. Apart from the parks and gardens on the itineraries, they include the Jardí de les Hesperides (located next to the Botanica Garden), planted with cypresses, palms and citrus trees, and the ambitious Parc de Cabecera at the top end of the River Túria. It houses the Bioparc, a zoo that breeds threatened species, a lake and, soon, a funfair. Opening times are daily 10am– 6pm (winter) and until 8pm (summer).

SPORT

Adventure Sports and Excursions: Centro Excursionista de Valencia, Pl Tavernes de La Valldigna 4, tel: 96 391 16 43. Excellent walking and cycling excursions. Kalahari Aventuras S.L., Mar 47, tel: 96 377 44 44 (www.kalahariadventures.com). Adventure sports outside the city.

Sailing: In 2007 the 32nd America's Cup was held in Valencia – the first time that it had been held in Europe.

The Club Naútico de Valencia, which arranges temporary berthing and membership, is best contacted via its website: www.rcnauticovalencia.com.

Golf: There are two outstanding courses: El Saler (tel: 96 161 11 86), ranked among Europe's best, often hosts the Spanish Open and is attached to a seaside state-owned hotel 20km (12 miles) outside the city, and the Escorpión (tel: 96 160 12 11). If these are too expensive try El Bosque (tel: 96 180 80 00) and Manises (tel: 96 152 18 71). All courses are open to non-members, although the handicap required and the green fees vary considerably. All courses hire out golf clubs.

Football: Camp de Mestalla is home to Valencia, one of the country's top teams. Ticket office tel: 96 393 71 26. Tickets cost €20–72, more for big matches. The second

Above: underwater tunnel at the spectacular L'Oceanogràfic *(see page 30)*

team, Levante, plays at the 25,000-seat Ciutat de Valencia stadium and tickets cost €20–30 from the stadium or club offices on the Alameda.

Trinquet: Local sports include this glove-free variant of Basque *pelota* played with taped hands. A visit to Bar Trinquet Pelayo, Pelayo 6, after 5.30pm from Wed to Sat, with largely male clientele, is a fun place to soak up the local atmosphere.

BEACHES

The city's beaches running north from the port are Las Arenas (also called Levante) and Malva Rosa, and to the north of that are those of Alboraia. They have the fun atmosphere of a city beach. To the south are El Pinedo, where there is a nudist beach, and El Saler. Both these hold blue flags. Part of El Saler lies within the Albufera natural park and is backed by pine trees and dunes, but there are also hotels here. Further south the beach runs down to Perelló, which has summer apartments and is more crowded.

Above: beach volleyball
Right: flowers feature in many festivals

USEFUL ADDRESSES

Tourist Offices
Pl de la Reina, 19 baix, tel: 96 315 39 31. The town hall's office (Mon–Fri 9am–7pm, Sat and Sun 10am–2pm).
Poeta Querol s/n (Teatro Principal), tel: 96 351 49 07. The Diputació office offers excellent information on the city and province (Mon–Fri 9.30am–7pm, Sat 10am–2pm, Sun 11am–2pm).
Pau (Paz) 48, tel: 96 398 64 22. The Generalitat's office, with information about the whole Valencian region (Mon–Fri 9am–8pm, Sat 10am–8pm, Sun 10am–2pm).
Estació del Nord, tel: 96 352 85 73. Office at the railway station (Mon–Fri 9am–6.30pm).
Turespaña National enquiries line with French and English speakers, toll free tel: 900 130 06 00.

Consulates
The main tourist office in Poeta Querol will be able to provide you with a list of the city's 37 consulates. They include:
British Consulate, Colom (Colón) 22, 5-H, tel: 96 352 07 10 (Mon–Fri 9am–1.30pm, 4.30–7pm); **US Consulate**, Dóctor Romagosa 1, 2-J, tel: 96 351 69 73 (Mon–Fri, 10am–1pm); **French Consulate**, Cronist Carreres 11, 1A, tel: 96 351 03 59 (Mon–Fri 9.30am–1pm); **German Consulate**, Avd Marqués de Sotelo 3–6, tel: 96 310 62 51 (Mon–Fri 9am–1pm).

FURTHER READING

Berlitz Guide Valencia, Apa Publications, 2008.
The Fabled Shore, Rose Macaulay, Oxford University Press, 1986.
Guía Azul – Valencia, Guía Azules de Espana SA, Maria Dolores Gijón and Paloma Ledredo, 2002.
Guía de la ciudad de Valencia. María Ángeles González Gudino, Del Senia al Segura 1998.
Insight Guide Spain, Apa Publications, 2008.
The New Spaniards, John Hooper, Penguin 1995.
Spain. A History. Ed. Raymond Carr, Oxford University Press, 2000.

ACKNOWLEDGEMENTS

Photography by Gregory Wrona/Apa
except:

10, 13	**Archivo Iconografico SA/Corbis**
12 (top and bottom)	**akg-images London**
15 (bottom)	**Swim Ink 2, LLC/Corbis**
41, 89	**Expuesto – Nicolas Randall/Alamy**
28	**Kevin Foy/Alamy**
46	**Miguel Raurich/Iberimage**
52	**Emma Lee/Life File/gettyimages**
64	**Jochem D. Wijnards/image bank/ gettyimages**
Cover	**Marco Cristofori/Corbis**

INDEX